Studies in Public Choice

Volume 38

More information about this series at http://www.springer.com/series/6550

David J. Hebert • Diana W. Thomas
Editors

Emergence, Entanglement, and Political Economy

Springer

Editors
David J. Hebert
Aquinas College
Grand Rapids, MI, USA

Diana W. Thomas
Creighton University
Omaha, NE, USA

ISSN 0924-4700
Studies in Public Choice
ISBN 978-3-030-56087-4 ISBN 978-3-030-56088-1 (eBook)
https://doi.org/10.1007/978-3-030-56088-1

This Springer imprint is published by the registered company Springer Nature Switzerland AG
The registered company address is: Gewerbestrasse 11, 6330 Cham, Switzerland

Contents

Contributors

Abigail Devereaux Wichita State University, Wichita, KS, USA

David J. Hebert Aquinas College, Grand Rapids, MI, USA

Jeremy Horpedahl University of Central Arkansas, Conway, AR, USA

Adam Martin Texas Tech University, Lubbock, TX, USA

Marta Podemska-Mikluch Gustavus Adolphus College, St. Peter, MN, USA

Alexander William Salter Texas Tech University, Lubbock, TX, USA

Diana W. Thomas Creighton University, Omaha, NE, USA

Michael D. Thomas Creighton University, Omaha, NE, USA

Meg Patrick Tuszynski Southern Methodist University, Dallas, TX, USA

Richard E. Wagner George Mason University, Fairfax, VA, USA

Introduction

David J. Hebert and Diana W. Thomas

Abstract This chapter is the editors' introduction to *Emergence, Entanglement, and Political Economy* and includes some overarching themes connecting the chapters of this volume.

Keywords Political economy · Spontaneous order, Public choice

In our day to day lives, we transition more or less fluently between many different institutional settings. Just considering the editors of this book, who are, to be fair, both academic economists and therefore lead much less interesting lives than most, we can come up with at least ten different communities and groups we are part of: we are teachers, researchers, and colleagues, on a university campus, we are members of a family in which we are each both parents and spouses, we are both members of church communities, we accompany our children to sports team activities outside of the home, we are shoppers at grocery stores and in malls, we are drivers on the road during morning and evening commute times, we are friends to people in the different communities we are part of, we are neighbors to the people who live near us, and we are siblings and children of families we came from. If you find yourself reading this book, you may be much like us in the sense that you are a member or participant in many different groups or institutional environments. Much like us, you will probably agree that despite the fact that you wear many hats your behavior and actions vary little, irrespective of the institutional setting you find yourself in. You have the same set of goals and aspirations irrespective of whether you are at work, at church, or at home. This basic insight that human behavior is relatively unchanged across different institutional environments is usually credited to James Buchanan and Gordon Tullock (1964) and known as behavioral symmetry.

D. J. Hebert (✉)
Aquinas College, Grand Rapids, MI, USA
e-mail: david.hebert@aquinas.edu

D. W. Thomas
Creighton University, Omaha, NE, USA
e-mail: dianathomas@creighton.edu

D. J. Hebert, D. W. Thomas (eds.), *Emergence, Entanglement, and Political Economy*, Studies in Public Choice 38, https://doi.org/10.1007/978-3-030-56088-1_1

Writing after the rise of welfare economics in the discipline, Buchanan and Tullock (1964) made the simple observation that in modeling politicians as benevolent welfare maximizers who could overcome the problems created by rationally self-interested actors in the context of market institutions, economists were committing what has come to be known as the Nirvana fallacy, i.e. the fallacy of comparing actual things with unrealistic, idealized alternatives. Born was public choice, or the study of non-market decision making, as it was initially known by its earliest proponents.

Public choice introduced a level of realism into the analysis of politics that has offered much profound and insightful scholarship. Economists arguably understand the political context of market decision making better today than they did before Buchanan and Tullock put pen to paper. And yet, as we and the other contributors to this volume will argue, to stop at behavioral symmetry would be missing the forest for the trees. While Public Choice scholars improved on the analytical accuracy of political economy models by demanding behavioral symmetry, they continued to treat politics and markets as fundamentally different realms of human action albeit populated by behaviourally similar actors.

Rather than assuming such stringent institutional boundaries, the contributors to this volume treat markets and politics (and for all intents and purposes all other human choice arenas) as fundamentally entangled. To offer a tangible example, one of your editors, Thomas, decided to switch to a local privately-owned pharmacy, which happens to be owned by a family in the parish she attends, after several unpleasant interactions with the staff of one of the big name retail pharmacy chains in her neighborhood. Our preferences and choices in one institutional setting, are contingent on and fundamentally interdependent with our choices and experiences in other areas of our lives.

Because human action in different institutional settings is so entangled and interdependent, analytically accurate models of human behavior have to focus on the emergent nature of the patterns we observe in political economy.

The title of this volume indicates two of the main ideas that are more fully utilized by the authors than are used by more traditional scholars. "Emergence" pushes back on the notion that outcomes observed within the political sphere are the designs of one centralized mind. Rather than view political outcomes as somehow intentional, the authors here recognize that these outcomes emerge from a competitive process that includes several different people operating within a specific framework of rules. For example, as explored by Jeremy Horpedahl, the tax code is not an object of choice for any particular legislator but is instead an amalgamation of different and often disparate interests over time.

"Entanglement" recognizes an old tenet of non-market decision making (the original name of Public Choice): behavioral symmetry. To summarize the insights contained here, any decision that results from a political entity must be the product of individual decision makers operating within some framework of formal and informal rules. To treat these decisions as if they were the product of one single mind, or even simply the additive result of several decisions, is to fundamentally misunderstand and mischaracterize the topic or issue being studied in two ways:

First, it mischaracterizes the topic in that it presumes some sort of rationality or intentionality of a group when, as several scholars have pointed out, is neither rationality nor intentionality can be simply assumed at the group level. Group preferences need not follow any sort of rational calculus; intransitivity of preferences abounds, for example. Taking this insight further, this mischaracterization of group action as rational and intentional lends itself to viewing statecraft as an engineering or technical exercise, to borrow Buchanan (1964)'s colorful illustration of how technical and economic efficiency, as they are traditionally defined, are really one and the same.

Second, it ignores the problems of a lack of residual claimancy. In private affairs, the importance of property rights is readily apparent and well-understood. Even in group settings in the private realm, the issue of residual claimancy is resolved through various mechanisms, e.g. shareholders and limited liability arrangements. In public affairs, however, such residual claimancy is utterly lacking. Thus, it is not any one person or group's fault when, e.g. budgets fail to balance, projects fail to be completed on time, or even, as Wagner and Eusepi (2017) elucidate, issues surrounding public debt arise.

Instead, there is no antimony between activities classified as "public" and "private" as there is in the Samuelsonian tradition. Instead, all activity is understandable through the lens of economics, with differences lying in the available strategies, incentives, and feedback mechanisms. In other words, a person who wishes to accomplish a given task has before them the option of doing so through the private sphere or through the public sphere and, assuming individual rationality, will select the least-cost option.

Further, to treat public and private as if they were separable is understood to be a fiction within this framework. Instead, the actions of people in the public sphere depend on the actions of people in the private sphere and vice versa. It is not as if the public sphere simply appends changes onto the private sphere as is traditionally argued though often not explicitly.

Richard Wagner provides the first essay in this volume, discussing entangled political economy as opposed to viewing politics and economy as separable entities. In doing so, he provides a brief outline of the two theories and also brings into play the concept of political profit and the primacy of examining the institutional features of public law.

The chapters by David Hebert and Abigail Deveraux present two new, but interrelated ways of viewing the political process. The chapter by Hebert brings system theory into view, arguing that using systems theory and a parts-to-whole framework provides a more cogent explanation of political outcomes observed today Deveraux brings to bear developments in complexity theory, agent based modeling, and artificial intelligence. She then applies Hayekian insights in discussing relevant issues in public choice and scholarship in political economy.

Two of the chapters discuss the language and analytical focus of entangled political economy: Marta Podemska-Mikluch discusses entrepreneurship from a means-oriented perspective as opposed to the ends-oriented one that dominates the literature today. In doing so, her chapter argues that rather than looking at the efficiency of an outcome of entrepreneurial activity, we should instead investigate the exchange patterns that emerge and whether they were voluntary or coerced. Adam Martin's chapter provides a brilliant explanation of how talk matters in political economy, not only in the sense that it conveys information between people but also communicates and constructs judgements about performance, values, and ultimately behavior.

The chapters by Tuszynski and Horpedahl discuss at length how the theory of emergent orders fits within the subject of political economy and helps explain the conditions under which a spontaneous order might result in a final outcome that leaves virtually all participants less than satisfied. Tuszynski applies her insights case of the public aid system in the United States, which is an important topic in today's world. Horpedahl focuses on tax codes and their complexity and discusses the challenges with aligning tax reforms with ideas understood and largely agreed upon by public finance scholars.

Alex Salter's chapter provides a survey and extension of the property rights literature by discussing political property rights as decision-making power. In doing so, his chapter highlights how market participants can, through lobbying efforts, effectively secure property rights to the market itself and how political enterprises assert their own property right to the market by acting as a form of gatekeeper into the specific industry that did the lobbying.

The chapter by Diana and Michael Thomas offers the evolution of state budgets and revenue systems over time as an example of an emergent political outcome that is undesirable from the perspective of the individuals comprising the whole and yet the result of individual action at the local, state, and federal government level over time. They argue that federal fiscal and tax institutions are set up to produce increasing levels of debt over time and a trend of shifting responsibility from the local through the state to the federal government.

This volume emerged out of discussions among several scholars at various conference sessions all working within the Austrian and Public Choice traditions on issues related to political economy. The successes that the scholars included here have had lies in their application of spontaneous order theorizing (Hayek) to contemporary issues in political economy. We wish to thank participants at the 2018 Southern Economic Conference and Society for the Development of Austrian Economics meetings and the 2019 Public Choice Society Meetings for their contributions to the volume as well as their feedback on earlier drafts of the chapters. None of this would be possible without the vigorous and spirited debate that conferences allow. The idea behind this volume is to showcase the next generation of scholars within this unique combination of traditions. In order for there to be a "next generation," there must be a "current generation." While there are several scholars that work in a similar tradition, to our mind, the current generation is best exemplified by the scholarship of Richard Wagner. That being said, this volume is not a festschrift to Wagner, but rather each chapter serves as an extension and application of the approach that he has been championing for years. Each of the authors in this volume have, at one time or another, worked closely with Wagner during their graduate studies and beyond. In fact, several have even co-authored with him.

The chapters in this collection very nicely reflect the ways in which the scholars of the next generation in the growing entangled political economy tradition are producing new insights and applications. They do this by acknowledging the contributions of the current and past generations and mixing them with the related contributions from other traditions and apply them to contemporary issues in political economy. This volume spans an impressive range of topics and ways of applying and integrating these insights and lays out new directions for the future of the field. We are proud to have helped assemble these chapters together and bring them to publication.

Emergence and Entanglement in a Theory of Political Economy

Richard E. Wagner

Abstract Political economy is a field of study where theorists typically treat polities and markets as separate orders of activity within society. Moreover, the standard mode of analysis treats those entities as existing in states of equilibrium. In contrast, this essay treats polities and markets as entangled and, moreover, as entities that have ecological and emergent character. Among other things, this shift in analytical focus means that turbulence of variable intensity is a key feature to be incorporated into a theory of political economy. It also means that human population systems are open and not closed, which further means that the future is generated through complex interaction inside a societal arena that entails both trade and conflict.

Keywords Entangled political economy · Emergence vs. axiomatics · Action level vs. systems level · Non-logical action · Indeterminism and creativity

JEL Codes D72 · D78 · E62 · H61 · P16

Political economy is a field of study where theorists typically treat polities and markets as separate orders of activity within society. Within this common scheme of thought, moreover, human action follows a temporal sequence, with economic action preceding political action. Where some theorists treat political action as correcting market failures, other theorists treat political action as creating market failures. Where orthodox welfare economics treats the political level as a locus of planning that Power inserts into society, public choice theorizing mostly claims that those planners are more self-interested than benevolent but maintains the distinction between levels of action and societal consequences. In contrast, this paper disputes the coherence of imposing different levels of action on our schemes of thought. Consequently, the compound noun "political economy" no longer refers to some relationship between two distinct levels of human activity within society, but rather

R. E. Wagner (✉)
George Mason University, Fairfax, VA, USA
e-mail: rwagner@gmu.edu

D. J. Hebert, D. W. Thomas (eds.), *Emergence, Entanglement, and Political Economy*, Studies in Public Choice 38, https://doi.org/10.1007/978-3-030-56088-1_2

refers to different carriers of action inside society. In this respect, I present an alternative societal topography where all action apprehended within a theory of political economy occurs on the same level.

Any scheme of thought emphasizes some phenomena and suppresses others. This situation holds for political economy just as strongly as it holds for other fields of study. In contrast to conventional thinking, I explain that the systems level cannot be entered directly, but can be entered only at the action level. The systems level is just a collection of statistics, projections, and reflections of beliefs, hopes, and ideologies. It is not, however, a place where action occurs. The systems level is a construction of the imagination, and the observations that pertain to that construction are generated through interaction among the individual entities that populate and comprise the system. In any case, we should keep in mind that in the social sciences we create what we observe. No one has ever truly observed the entities we denote as polity or economy in their entireties, as against observing parts and pieces of those entities. Our observations necessarily constructed through acts of theorization, regarding which choices exist.

While numerous choices are possible in this respect, these can reasonably be reduced to two categories depending on how the theoretical foregrounds and backgrounds are populated. Most political economy places in the analytical foreground systemic structure using presumptions of equilibrium and methods of comparative statics applied to holistic entities. It is not that those theorists necessarily believe this is the way the world looks, but rather think it is a useful way of looking at it all the same. We all necessarily employ concepts of equilibrium, regularity, and pattern in our thinking to navigate our way in the world. There is, however, an open question regarding the relation between foreground and background with respect to our theoretical constructions. This essay reverses foreground and background from conventional analytical portraits. Brought into the analytical foreground are individual action inside the holistic entities that populate most thinking on political economy. This alternative foreground emphasizes the continual emergence of new material into political economy, and with that emergence set in motion by individual action inside the entities that are normally taken as the units of observation. For any theoretical schema, it is always good to remember that old aphorism: the proof of any pudding lies always in the eating.

1 A Societal Topography: Action Level and Systems Level

The most common view of political economy, which Persson and Tabellini (2000) and Drazen (2002) illustrate, treats the compound noun "political economy" as constructed by addition over distinct arenas of activity: PE = P + E. Figure 1 describes this conceptual framework. Society is conceptualized as holding two distinct entities: an economy and a polity. An economy is further regarded as an equilibrated set of interactions and relationships, much as portrayed by claims on behalf of general equilibrium theory of the dynamic and stochastic variety. That economy is reduced

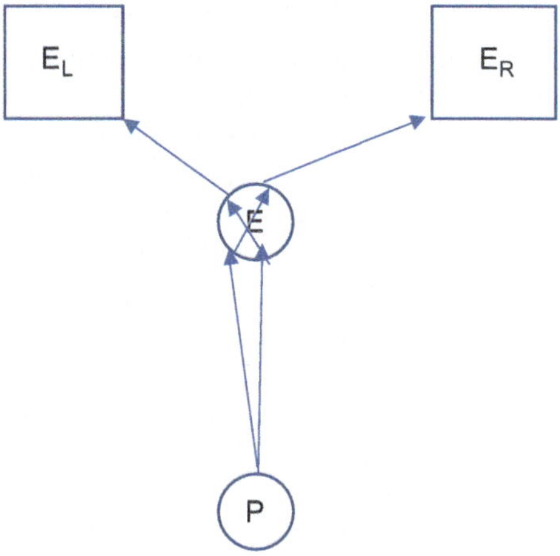

Fig. 1 Additive political economy: PE = P + E

to a point-mass entity by the widely used presuppositions of a general equilibrium that is dynamic and stochastic (DSGE), though Fig. 1 expands that point to the circle denoted by E to make it visible.

Lying south of E is the political entity P. Within democratic polities, that entity contains a variety of positions, offices, and powers that candidates compete to possess for some interval of time until the next election. Those candidates and parties compete for the support of voters by offering programs they hope will resonate more strongly with voters than the programs opposing candidates offer. To be sure, there are differences among models in how the relationship between candidates and voters is conceptualized. Some models treat votes as having hard-wired preferences, with candidates seeking to locate in the center of the distribution of preferences. Other models treat voter preferences as having significant elements of openness, with candidates seeking to articulate images that resonate particularly strongly with voters.

For some analytical purposes, different approaches to conceptualizing the relationship between candidate positions and voter desires is analytically significant. For purposes of this paper, however, this difference is inconsequential. What is consequential is the separation between polity and economy in political economy. Figure 1 shows political economy as similar to playing pool. An economy E is like an object ball, and competing candidates are offering to shift that ball to different locations on the table, as denoted by EL and ER. Without doubt, this theoretical vision offers us some traction in apprehending the world of experience. Candidates do compete to win elections, and they make speeches regarding their plans and aspirations in their efforts to win the election.

In this paper I do not challenge this portrait. To the contrary, I accept it, only I relegate it to the analytical background, bringing forward in the process what is set aside in the portrait that Fig. 1 offers. I do this because what is set aside in such constructions as Fig. 1 is of great human significance, so should not be dropped from view simply because it has no place within the DSGE set of analytical conventions. To bring that material into analytical view requires use of some framework grounded on emergence, evolution, and entanglement, all of which are ignored by the DSGE framework.

Figure 2 offers a visual distinction between the systems level and the action level and does so within the context of standard macro theory, and with Wagner (2012) developing a similar figure. The systems level is portrayed in terms of aggregate supply and demand to keep contact with macro theory. It is important to note, however, that action does not occur at the systems level. Action can occur only at the action level, regardless of whether that action is undertaken by market or by political entities. All action and changes in actions are initiated by entities on the action level. The societal impact of those actions depends on their effects on other entities on the action level, as illustrated by the various patterns of connection among those entities.

Figure 2 differs from Fig. 1 in at least two notable respects. For one thing, neither polity nor economy is reduced to some point-mass entity. To the contrary, both polity and economy are treated as ordered sets of relationships and interactions among

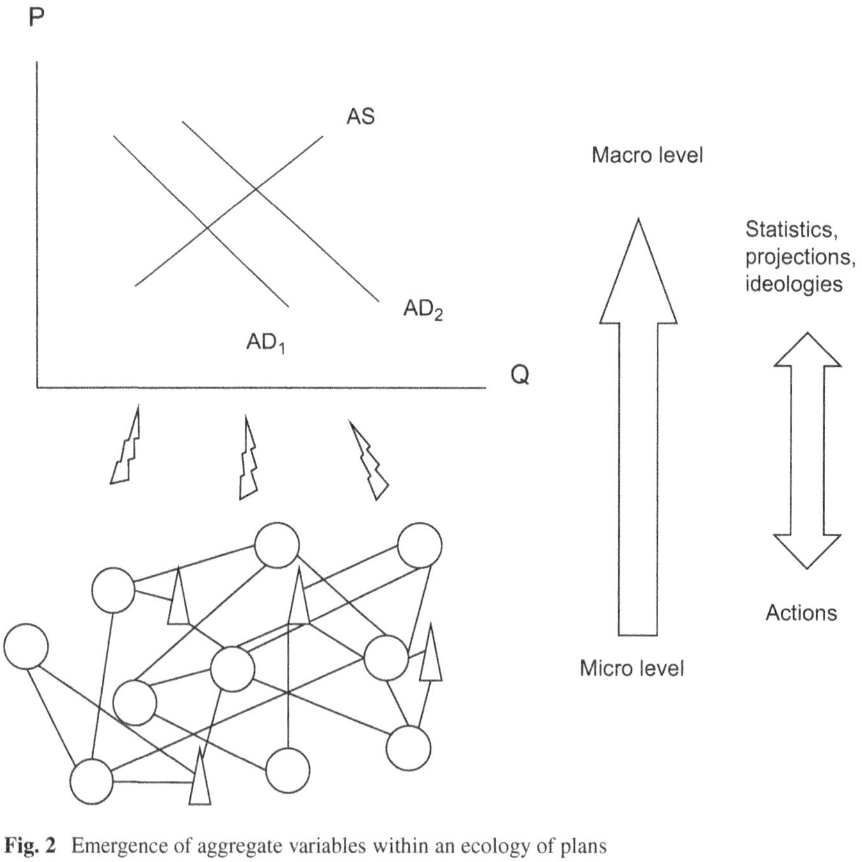

Fig. 2 Emergence of aggregate variables within an ecology of plans

various entities. Figure 1 shows polity as inserting planning into a market economy, changing the market's configuration in the process. Figure 2, by contrast, shows political action as a vector of activities and not as some such scalar force as a billiard ball. Just as an economy is an order and not an organization, so is a polity an order and not an organization. The lower part of Fig. 2 describes an order of organizations, some political and some economic, with the outcome of that system depending on patterns of interaction among the entities within the system.

The second notable feature of Fig. 2 is the entanglement between political and economic entities. Political entities do not act independently of market entities, in contrast to what Fig. 1 portrays. Figure 2 illustrates a situation where political entities require cooperation from some market-based entities just as market entities require support from some political entities. The inputs that enter a firm's production function are not fully it's choice to make because in many ways it will need to assemble politically-supplied inputs. Similarly, supporters of the political enterprises depicted in Fig. 2 will require support from some of the market-based enterprises in Fig. 2.

To speak of cooperation between political enterprises and market enterprises is not to assert that cooperation is mutually beneficial. In this regard, Marta Podemska-Mikluch and Richard Wagner (2013) distinguish between dyadic and triadic exchange. Market exchanges are dyadic, no matter how numerous the participants. The essence of dyadic exchange is its voluntariness because market institutions and practices operate through agreement. In contrast, democratic polities feature triadic exchanges to reflect the democratic principle of majority rule. The basic mode of majority rule is two people forming an agreement and to include a third party in that agreement to bear costs that the other two are unwilling to bear. With triadic exchanges, market entities are on both sides of a politically-sponsored transaction: there are allies of the political sponsor who gain from the deal and there are opponents who lose, and with those losses being the means by which the majority gains.

2 Entanglement in a Theory of Political Economy

Figure 3 formalizes the vision of political economy that corresponds to the bi-level societal topography that Fig. 2 illustrates and does so in a manner consistent with principles of emergence and entanglement. To be sure, Fig. 3 is nominally more concerned with analytical structure that with evolution and emergence. On the surface, Fig. 3 is a standard representation of the production frontier for a society. Output is distributed between political output and market output. These outputs are described by the scalar measures G and M, though we should recognize that our objects of interest, G and M, are both vectors of activities. Within the DSGE framework, the vector of market activities can be reduced to a scalar measure, M; the presumption that all observations pertain to states of equilibrium mean that market prices can reduce the entire array of market outputs to such a scalar measure as privately-generated GDP. To be sure, this reduction of a vector of activities to a

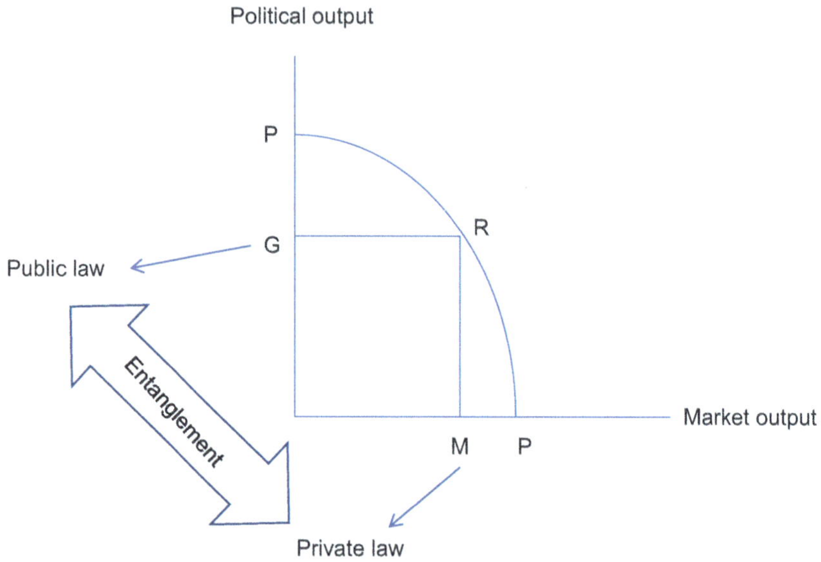

Fig. 3 Explanation in political economy: mapping analytical challenges

scalar is dubious outside the presupposition that all observations pertain to states if equilibrium.

This analysis is straightforward with respect to the aggregate of market-generated output, given acceptance of the DSGE presumptions. The treatment of political output is not at all straightforward. Indeed, it is an act of fantasy that is undertaken to maintain analytical symmetry with the analysis of market output. To reduce the vector of political activities to the scalar measure G is a piece of mythology that enables completion of Fig. 3. Political output is observable as a vector of activities, but political transactions do not generate prices for political output, so that vector cannot be reduced to a scalar, other than by undertaking some sleight of hand. One common sleight of hand is to postulate a social welfare function that assigns weights to the individual objects of political supply. To be sure, such weights are fictional with respect to political output. In contrast, market prices provide some semblance of weights for aggregating market output, although it is certainly a fictional presumption to claim that equilibrium prices remain unchanged throughout the accounting period to which the measure of M pertains.

As Fig. 3 is commonly presented, it is terribly misleading. The common presentation shows only M and G and it suppresses the three subtended concepts: private law, public law, and entanglement. When those subtended variables are left aside, Fig. 3 appears to claim that "societies" face choices of how to deploy inputs in the production of political and market output. There is nothing abjectly wrong with this common presentation, other than its being terribly misleading. To start, societies don't face choices. Individuals and organizations inside those societies face choices. Those choices, moreover, are always of particular activities, and most certainly not the aggregative-type variables denoted as M and G. Those aggregative variables M and G are not objects that any person chooses. To the contrary, they emerge through complex patterns of interaction among everyone who participates in generating market and political output.

In no way is it a useful or helpful language to speak of a society as "choosing" how to allocate resources between market output and political output. Indeed, such acts of choice are impossible with anything remotely approaching contemporary levels of societal complexity. Paul Craig Roberts (1971) explained that the Soviet Union was never the centrally planned economy that the textbooks explained it as being. To the contrary, the Soviet Union was polycentric and not monocentric, only it was a terribly fouled up instance of polycentricity. In a monocentric arrangement, all entities but one experience life as a puppet manipulated by a puppeteer. Puppets have no domain of autonomous action. The liberal ideal of a market economy is highly polycentric in that all actions entail agreement among participants. The Soviet Union operated with vast domains of privilege and force, which were responsible for its debilitating economic character, but it still unavoidably entailed zones of autonomous action of limited scope.

Subtended to M and G in Fig. 3 are two institutional variables denoted as private law and public law. It is with respect to these variables where the significant analytical work must be done. For now, focus on the market output side of Fig. 3. This is the domain of the economic theory of a market economy. That theory is normally described as a theory of price and allocation. It is, however, misleading to place pricing and allocation in the analytical foreground. Prices are not just there; they are not primitive variables for economic analysis. Prices emerge out of individual searches for profitable transactions. What makes those transactions possible is the ability of people to own and exchange objects. Until the eighteenth century in much of the west, for instance, landed property could not be subdivided but had to pass in tact upon the owner's death to the eldest son under primogeniture. The abolition of primogeniture made possible the emergence of a market in real estate.

The variable denoted by M in Fig. 3 is not an object of choice but is rather a summary of the complex array of activities that people undertake within the institutional framework associated with the private ordering of economic activity. The most significant feature of the theory of a market economy is its ability to facilitate and accommodate complex patterns of economic organization that could not be attained through any form of planning outside of market interaction. While the theory of markets is commonly described as price and allocation theory, that theory is not a type of handbook for planners. It does not provide guidance for planners on how to construct socially beneficial outcomes. To the contrary, the theory illuminates the internal logic of the institutional framework denoted as private law.

The theory of a market economy explains how it is possible that a coherent pattern of economic activity can emerge inside a society even though that pattern is not the creation of any person or office inside society. To the contrary, that pattern is generated through people pursuing opportunities for mutual gain when human interactions are governed by the legal institutions associated with private law, namely private property, freedom of contract, and personal liability for choices. While the logic of market theory runs in terms of prices and allocations, the foreground of the theory rests on the private ordering of human interaction.

3 Public Law and Public Economy

Vito Tanzi (2011) observes that a century or so ago politically determined output was around 10% of total output throughout the western lands. A theory of a market economy could serve as a first-order approximation for a theory of the entirety of economic activity. An analytical focus on the notion of an unhampered market economy could plausibly have been said to provide a reasonable approximation to the entire economy. What might have been set aside by ignoring the remaining 10% of economic activity would surely have seemed small in the overall scheme of things. The conceptual innocence entailed in ignoring political activity is no longer excusable when political output throughout the western lands has expanded from around 10% to around 40% and even more of total output since early in the twentieth century.

Even more, political output is not captured by budgetary magnitudes alone. Whatever impact on resource allocation a polity can achieve through its budget can be achieved through regulatory requirements. On a small scale, local governments could reduce or even eliminate their spending on snow removal by requiring property owners to clear streets and sidewalks adjacent to their property. I doubt if anyone would think this change desirable, due among other things to differences in the speed at which patches of road would be cleared, but it does offer a small-scale illustration of the substitutability between taxes and regulations in achieving allocative outcomes. On a larger scale, jurisdictions could abolish their budgets for elementary and secondary education by requiring parents to send their children to approved schools.

In our modern world, there is surely merit in seeking to develop explanatory accounts of political activity. The form such a theory would take seems clear by referring to Fig. 3. G denotes a scalar in Fig. 3, and yet it really represents a vector of politically sponsored activities. With respect to the lower part of Fig. 2, all the triangles shown there sponsor various activities that are aggregated into G in Fig. 3. This move from individual political entities in Fig. 2 to aggregate political output in Fig. 3 conceals far more than it reveals about political economy. Subtended to G in Fig. 3 is the institutional variable denoted as "public law," which is the political complement to private law in the theory of a market economy.

With respect to the institutions of private law, we have a good idea informed by more than two centuries of economic theorizing as to how a set of people in pursuit of beneficial transactions generate market prices and resource allocations that we can summarize as M in Fig. 3. By contrast, we have little idea of how people pursuing beneficial transactions inside political contexts framed by the institutions and practices of public law generate patterns of political output that can be summarized by G in Fig. 3. When G was around one-tenth the magnitude of M this theoretical omission might not have been terrible significant. But when the two magnitudes are similar, we seem surely to have a gaping hole in our theory of political economy.

Further complexity is added by the double arrow labeled entanglement that runs between public law and private law in Fig. 3. Without that arrow and the entanglement it denotes, markets and polities would operate as independent arenas of action within society. This situation would be similar to monarchical times, provided kings could not impose taxes without obtaining the consent of those being taxed. Such independence between political and economic entities does not exist, nor is it clear how it might. During feudal times, there were royal families and ordinary common families, and people did not move between those designations. Within democratic times, however, a person can engage simultaneously in political action and in market action. A person who starts life as a business person can run for political office. After 20 years in politics, a person might retire and move into business.

One could even do both at the same time, as illustrated by the eminent Italian theorist of public finance, Antonio de Viti de Marco who served for 20 years as a member of the Italian parliament while also serving as a professor of public finance at the University of Rome. The most significant feature about entanglement in political economy is the presence of permeable boundaries between polity and economy. A person might establish a business within the market, and yet might seek to sell services to political enterprises. That same person, moreover, might support particular politicians and their programs over other politicians and programs. One aspect of a political program might entail support for restrictions on the reach of private ordering by restricting the domain to which principles of free association pertain.

In contemporary times, any effort to treat a theory of production in substantive fashion as against treating it in purely formal fashion will necessarily recognize that production will require the assembly of politically-supplied inputs in addition to assembling inputs through market transactions. Despite entanglement, private law has something that public law needs but cannot generate on its own: market prices. Market prices emerge in the presence of alienable property rights. Land could not carry market prices in the days of primogeniture. Market prices are essential tools for assisting in the generation of coordinated patterns of economic activity (Boettke 2001). For small-scale societies of tribal size, social coordination can be arranged through some conjunction of custom and leadership (Schmookler 1984). For modern societies, however, coordination through prices and market transactions is inescapable, though political power can always be deployed to restrict the scope for market exchange (Roberts 1971).

4 Parasitical Politics and Economic Calculation

Figure 4 conveys what I mean in saying that private law has something that public law lacks but needs. Fig. 4 is two figures combined into one. The first figure contains five clusters of large and small circles. The five clusters are distributed across some abstract commodity space and indicate positions where entrepreneurs have

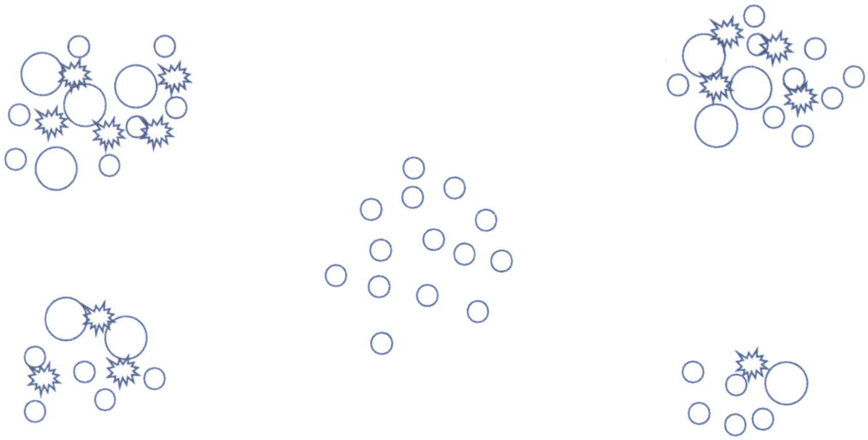

Fig. 4 Political-economic interaction within abstract commodity space

established enterprises. These clusters are analogous to different commodity groups or, alternative, to different places where prospectors have chosen to locate. The center of Fig. 4 shows a relatively large number of smaller enterprises. Descriptively, these might pertain to handicraft types of firms: yard care firms, house painting firms, residential remodeling, and the like.

The other four clusters contain a variable mix of larger and smaller firms. The northwest has the largest share of larger firms, with the northeast standing second in the share of larger firms. The point of reference, however, is not geographical but is commercial and industrial. The northwest, for instance, might denote heavy industry. The northeast might denote high concentrations of human capital. However specific context might be supplied, the analytical point of departure starts with recognition that a process of open market competition will generate a pattern of industrial organization that will reflect some underlying economic realities regarding different types of production processes and possible economies of interaction among similar types of producers.

The theory of open markets gives us insight into how economic activities are coordinated within this society. But how does politics enter this picture? Political enterprises do not sell services and are not subject to alienable property rights. Hence, political enterprises cannot generate prices to help in reaching judgments about resource allocation, nor can they reward executives based on changes in enterprise value. Nor, for that matter, can they offer to buy or sell enterprises or parts of enterprises. Alienable property rights which are essential to well-coordinated economic activity cannot be brought directly to bear on the coordination of political activity.

Public law lacks what is needed for political coordination, which suggests in turn a relation between markets and polities. That relation is injected into Fig. 4 through the jagged objects that are inserted near the various circles. Those jagged objects, moreover, are inserted in a systematic manner and most certainly not in some random fashion. In short, Fig. 4 is constructed on the proposition that political entities follow the actions of successful market enterprises by attaching themselves parasitically to those market enterprises (Pantaleoni 1911).

Pantaleoni conceptualized a society as containing two bazaars. The market bazaar was organized through market prices, which for Pantaleoni were equal to marginal costs of production. For Pantaleoni's desire to place public finance on an explanatory setting, he conceptualized the vendors within the political bazaar as charging political prices. At this point an unavoidable ambiguity is encountered. That ambiguity didn't face vendors in the market bazaar because prices were presumed to be technologically determined by input-output relationships in production. While such input-output relationships were also present in the political bazaar, political prices had an element of arbitrary volition that market prices lacked. Pantaleoni resolved this arbitrariness by assuming that political prices were established by a flat-rate of tax on all income.

This flat-rate tax meant that political prices rose directly with income, in contrast to market prices which were invariant to income. Obviously, vendors in the political bazaar would not be able to sell to buyers with above-average income without either prohibiting competing sales in the market bazaar or using other devices to lower the price. The system of political pricing does not serve the same coordinating function as market prices serve. It is market prices that serve that coordinating function for political enterprises, recognizing that political enterprises attach themselves parasitically to market prices and enterprises. I should perhaps stress that "parasitical" is used technically without normative shading. A parasite cannot live on its own, for it requires a host. A parasite might harm a host, but it might also benefit the host. The technical point is that parasites are supported by hosts.

Market enterprises participate in the generation of market prices which in turn help market enterprises to coordinate their activities with other market enterprises. Political enterprises do not generate any kind of price information that would prove valuable to those enterprises in conducting their operations or in changing their patterns of operation. Political enterprises latch onto market prices and market enterprises in navigating their way through the waters of a democratic political economy. The needle-like quality of the jagged objects in Fig. 4 illustrate parasitical political attachment to market outcomes. The largest number of political enterprises are in the northwest of Fig. 4. The explanation for this pattern must be that this is where political enterprises can capture the largest political profit. This explanation requires clarification because political enterprises are organized without transferable ownership and so are explicitly non-profit enterprises.

There are several reasons why sellers might bundle two or more items as a package rather than offering each item individually. One reason which seems particularly useful for thinking about the creation of profit within political enterprises is the use of tied sales to avoid price controls. The classic example is rent control, though examples abound. If rents are restricted to less than what people are willing to pay, those people will compete among themselves to attain their desired rental units. One possible method is for owners to tie the sale of furniture with acceptance of a rental contract. Should local authorities seek to restrict such tied sales, the situation remains one where there are more people seeking housing units than there are units available at the controlled price. Tenants will compete among themselves for space they desire, and that competition can manifest in such ways as rent-controlled apartments converting a freely available pool into a membership-only club. Alternatively, freely available garage space could now be leased as a separate transaction.

The general principle in play here is that political enterprises can extract profit from transactions they undertake, only that profit will be extracted through some entity that is not subject to price control. In this respect, political enterprises are subjected effectively to price control by virtue of their being non-profit entities. While the political enterprise may operate in a non-profit manner, that enterprise will engage in transactions with profit-seeking enterprises. It takes no unreasonable stretch of the imagination to see how an enterprise forced to operate in a non-profit fashion can extract profit through some of its contractual partners. To be sure, such profit can manifest in myriad ways of various degrees of venality. Setting aside concerns of venality, the simple fact of the matter is that gains from trade will surly be captured by enterprise executives in some fashion. Just what fashion is indefinite, but the existence of some such fashion is surely not, for failing to do so would be knowingly to walk away from what is effectively free money.

5 Working with Political Profit as a Concept

Marta Podemska-Mikluch and Richard Wagner (2013) distinguish between dyadic and triadic exchange within political economy. Their distinction is theoretical and abstract. It is not substantive. That is, the distinction does not concern the number of participants. It rather concerns the form of exchange relationships. The distinction between dyadic and triadic concerns the lowest number of participants who can be involved in an exchange for that exchange to retain its dyadic or triadic character. A dyadic exchange can involve thousands or millions of persons, as Richard Epstein (1995) notes in explaining how simple rules can organize incredibly complex situations.

The distinction between dyadic and triadic concerns the lowest number of persons necessary to reveal the central properties of an exchange relationship. The world of democratic political economy is organized through transactions, just as is the world of market interaction. The principles governing those transactions differs between the two environments. As Epstein (1995) explains, the liberal market principles of private property and freedom of contract can accommodate creation of incredibly complex transactions, disproving common claims that the increasing complexity of modern life requires an increasing growth of complex regulations. To the contrary, Epstein shows that simple rules suitable for voluntary participation in transactions can accommodate open-ended complexity.

For a dyadic exchange, the magic number is two. This magic number means that even the most complex of transactions can have its central properties illustrated by a trade between two people. All exchanges entail a mutual expectation of capturing gains from trade, and this situation can be illustrated by the simple Edgeworth box diagram that is a staple of the textbooks. Sure, actual exchanges will often include numerous provisions to deal with possible contingencies. For instance, a promoter might agree with a team owner to provide halftime entertainment at an event. The group that agreed with the promoter to provide the entertainment might have arrived ill-prepared or even late. This possibility and the bearing of the associated liabilities can be readily apprehended within the framework of dyadic exchange. So might a situation where the group arrives late or even not at all due to a strike by an air pilots association. Complex transactions can be grounded and constructed through negotiation and agreement.

For a triadic exchange, the magic number is three. The essential features of the political exchanges that form the core of democratic political economy, especially in larger governments without easy exit, require three participants to illustrate their essential features, and those features are built into the points of contract between the circles and the needle-nosed objects in Fig. 4. The magic number three is necessary to enable the supporters of a trading relationship to enhance their gains through their ability to transfer to other people some of the cost associated with that relationship. For instance, a political coalition might support a program to ignore pre-existing conditions when making actuarial estimates for an insurance program, when the alternative might have been to charge actuarial prices and incorporate support for those prices into a welfare budget. Instead, those conditions are ignored, which forces some people pay rates higher than what would be warranted on actuarial grounds. People in this position are on the outside of triadic exchanges, for it is their excess payments that finance the gains from trade that accrue to sponsors and beneficiaries of the program.

Profit is just a special case of gain. Both terms express the idea of mutual benefit, only gain extends to numerous instances of exchange that occur outside the ordinary world of commerce. Many people pay dues to clubs to which they belong. Those clubs nearly always are organized as non-profit entities. Yet we may be sure that people regard the dues they pay as being worthwhile, for otherwise we would expect them to drop their membership. We may likewise reasonably think that club officers think their service is worthwhile, for otherwise we may doubt that they would supply that service. In other words, mutual gain is a generally valid characteristic of trading relationships, whereas profit pertains to but a subset, though a significant subset, of trading relationships. All dyadic relationships entail the expectation of mutual gain, while only a subset of those relationships entail profit.

The difficulty with gain as a political concept is that it includes triadic and well as dyadic relationships. This triadic character, moreover, seems to be an especially durable feature of politically-organized relationships in the presence of significant exit costs. Spencer MacCallum (1970) explains lucidly how hotels and shopping centers incorporate the supply of public goods into their ordinary business activities. In this respect, a hotel is like a city. In both cases there are both private goods and public goods. Cities organize public goods within a triadic budgetary process. In contrast, hotels organize them through a network of dyadic exchanges where residents receive a tied bundle of private and public goods when they reside in a hotel.

The elevators in a hotel are subways that run vertically. Hotels provide public spaces of various types, choose how well to maintain their premises, and provide security services, among other types of publicly available services.

There seem generally to be two types of difference between cities and hotels, and only two, one relatively superficial and one more significant. The relatively superficial difference concerns the political character of cities in contrast to the market-based character of hotels. To describe this difference as superficial is not to describe it as insignificant. That difference is clearly significant, as any comparison of cities and hotels or shopping centers will quickly show. That difference, however, does not seem to reside in political organization per se. After all, clubs of all types are also political organizations, only they engage in dyadic and not triadic transactions.

This recognition that political organizations can engage in dyadic transactions leads one to ask how it is that some political settings center on dyadic transactions while others support triadic transactions. Surely a plausible answer to this question resides in the costliness members face in replacing one political unit with another. If the cost of replacement is low, sponsors of those political enterprises must strive continually to attract members and to retain those who they have previously attracted. This necessity to attract members limits the range of the terms of trade sponsors can insert into their environments. For hotels and shopping centers, the cost of exit is practically zero. About all that is involved is the time it takes to change hotels. Cities where people primarily are renters would seem to be in a similar position, with the only significant difference being the length of apartment leases.

It is with owner-occupied housing that exit costs become significant. One element of that cost is the necessity of selling a house, and perhaps buying another one in another city. Financially, those costs run in the range of 5% of the price of the house these days, while also typically entailing a significant amount of time to move from one locale to another. But financial costs are only the most visible form of cost. Among other elements of cost are what might be called affective costs. These refer to various emotional sentiments and ties that connect a person or persons to a particular place of residence. All of these are forms of locational rents, and such rents exist in a dialectical tension. On the one hand, rents are the sources of joy in life, for they speak to what is freely available as against being purchased through making tradeoffs across margins. On the other hand, rents open people to be exploited, as through being on the losing end of triadic exchanges.

As a general proposition, we can say that the ability of political organizers to support the extraction of rents varies directly with the cost of exit from the jurisdictions they manage. In this respect, the original American constitutional order not only featured small government in general but also featured mostly local government. The direction of movement within American political economy for well over a century has been the replacement of local with national activity, which led Michael Greve (2012) to describe the de facto American Constitution has having been turned upside down. The original American Constitution was founded both on securing competition among governments and on dividing and separating the political power that resided within the federal government. The direction of movement within the American constitutional system has been one where the federal government has served as the agent for cartelizing what had been a competitive system of governments, as such sources as Aligica and Tarko (2012), Boettke (2007), Epstein (2014), Holcombe (2002), Ostrom (1987, 1997), and Wagner (2006, 2014) explore.

6 From Wicksell to Buchanan and His Unfinished Analytical Agenda

Richard Wagner (2017) explains that pretty much the entire corpus of James Buchanan's scholarly work can be traced to the seeds contained within the first scholarly paper he published (Buchanan 1949). There, Buchanan contrasted organismic and individualistic approaches to public finance. By organismic, Buchanan included nearly the entire corpus of public finance wherein the state was treated as some goal-seeking entity. For those theorists, there was no significant difference between theorizing about the public finances of monarchies and theorizing about the public finances of democracies. For monarchies, there was a real person who directed the activities of state. For democracies, a real monarch was replaced by some such fictional notion as public interest, social contract, or social welfare function as these notions were guided by the propositions of welfare economics.

In contrast to the public finance theorizing of his time, Buchanan (1949) sketched the contours of what a theory of public finance might look like within a genuinely democratic regime. Most significantly for Buchanan, a genuinely democratic theory of public finance would operate through genuinely dyadic exchanges. How that might be accomplished is not an easy question to address, but Buchanan identified two prime sources of inspiration: Knut Wicksell (1896) and Antonio de Viti de Marco (1936). Wicksell set forth what later was translated (Wicksell 1958) as "A New Principle of Just Taxation." For Wicksell, justice in taxation required a quid pro quo between the taxes people paid and the values they placed on governmental activity. Similarly, de Viti de Marco (1888, 1936) distinguished between cooperative and monopolistic forms of democracy, with the cooperative form being similar to Wicksell's notion of just taxation. This way of thinking about public finance got underway at the end of the nineteenth century and became known as the benefit principle of public finance in its effort to treat state activity as having similar properties to the consumer sovereignty associated with market processes of economic organization. Indeed, de Viti referred to "tax-prices" to indicate a congruity between political and market activity, as Eusepi and Wagner (2013) note.

In his well-received review of the efforts by Wicksell (1896, 1958) and Erik Lindahl (1958 [1913]) to develop the benefit principle, Richard Musgrave (1939) asserted the impossibility of pursuing that development because he claimed people would not reliably reveal their preferences for political activity. In what became canonical papers in the theory of public goods, Paul Samuelson (1954, 1955) reinforced Musgrave's assertion. The Musgrave-Samuelson assertion held that public finance must necessarily be the domain of the arbitrary imposition of power because it was impossible to incorporate individual valuations of public activity into political outcomes. With respect to Fig. 3, market processes could reflect individual valuations, but political processes could not. Political outcomes could not be explained because they were arbitrary impositions by those who held political power. One might hope the holders of democratic power will be beneficent, but the use of that power will be the choice of the holder in any case.

In contrast to Musgrave and Samuelson, James Buchanan (1967, 1968) took several initial steps toward constructing a process-oriented explanation of political activity. Construction of that agenda remains unfinished, indeed, has barely begun. Buchanan explained that constructing such an approach to public finance required shifting the analytical focus away from resource allocations and placing it instead on the institutional and constitutional arrangements of governance. In other words, Buchanan moved the focus away from G in Fig. 3 and placed it on the institutional features denoted as public law. Whether a genuinely democratic theory of public finance predicated on the proposition that people establish governments to promote their common interests is conceivable reduces to the question of whether a substantive statement of public law in Fig. 3 can be set forth. Knut Wicksell (1896) took a major step in this direction. While Wicksell did not set forth a complete statement of public law, a consideration of Wicksell's scheme of thought along the lines that Wagner (1988) sketches will provide a useful framework for exploring this problematic of democratic political economy.

Wicksell is commonly summarized as declaring that the prime principle of democracy is unanimity and not majority rule (Buchanan and Tullock 1962). This summary is certainly accurate, though it is also incomplete as a perusal of the untranslated third essay in Wicksell (1896) will show. Wicksell thought democracy should reflect consensus and asked how that principle of consensus might be incorporated into Swedish institutions and practices. Among other things, a vote stands at the end of some political process. Much material of interest lies in the actions and activities that precede a vote. Wicksell recognized that unanimity would give everyone a veto over collective action, which could prevent many desirable activities from being undertaken. For this reason, Wicksell advanced such pragmatic rule as five-sixths, seven-eighths, and similarly highly inclusive rules. Beyond a voting rule, we may reasonably conclude that Wicksell thought of democracy as a process for governing through consensus among affected parties which could be illustrated by but not reduced to a voting rule.

In this respect, it is useful to consider briefly Wicksell's full contribution toward articulating a scheme of public law that would complement the market-affirming framework of private law. To start, Wicksell thought it violated liberal principles for people to be represented by people they opposed. The quality of being represented was substantive and not formal for Wicksell. To achieve this quality requires a system based on proportional representation, which in turn requires the selection of multiple candidates per voting district. How many candidates depends on presumptions about the extent of heterogeneity within the population. Wicksell presumed that Sweden was relatively homogeneous, so could be represented through a relative handful of political parties. The central presumption behind such proportional representation was that a parliament so selected could approximate a miniaturization of the Swedish society. To the extent this miniaturization was achieved, consensus within parliament would translate into consensus within Sweden.

With a parliament selected by proportional representation and faced with a highly qualified voting rule, the challenge becomes one of passing business through that parliament. Wicksell thought that Sweden could be reflected in miniature through a relative handful of political parties. Each party could sponsor legislation but would have to achieve concurrence from most if not all of the other parties to be successful. To operate in this fashion, it would be necessary for any proposed legislation to be accompanied by a proposal to cover the cost. In this way, the Swedish budgetary process would entail tax earmarking on a gigantic scale, with each proposal to spend money accompanied by a proposal to cover the cost. The motivational force behind this budgetary process was to render Swedish budgeting congruent with a substantive consent of the governed, in contrast to the purely formal notion that whatever government does reflects consent of the government because that is the way democratic governments inexorably operate.

Even more, Sweden had an executive in the form of a monarch. With parliament operating by a principle of near-unanimity, the monarch could fulfill the entrepreneurial position of recommending programs for parliamentary consideration, recognizing that such programs would be adopted only if they received nearly unanimous support from the members of parliament. This Wicksellian constitutional program reflects one particular approach to developing an institutional arrangement of public law that would complement the market-sustaining arrangement of private law.

The Italian theorist of public finance, Antonio De Viti de Marco (1888, 1936) thought along similar lines as Wicksell, only without entering into the institutional details that attracted Wicksell's attention. De Viti distinguished between two forms of democracy, which he denoted as cooperative and monopolistic. Cooperative democracy reflected the same consensual principle that animated Wicksell's ideal institutional framework. Monopolistic democracy illustrated the operation of democratic processes in the presence of high costs of exiting from political relationships. It is worth noting that de Viti spent 20 years as a member of the Italian parliament, elected from his home district near Lecce. In a collection of essays, de Viti de Marco (1930) chronicled 20 years of political struggle against the forces and processes of monopolistic democracy, indicating that de Viti though that the monopolistic model occupied the foreground of Italian political economy. Regardless of such matters, Wicksell, de Viti, and Buchanan all recognized that the challenge facing a genuinely democratic theory of public finance and political economy was institutional and constitutional in nature. In this recognition, these theorists tackled the "who guards the guardians" question from antiquity, only they approached it from the substantive direction of realistic institutional and constitutional provisions.

7 A Closing Comment

It is conventional to treat market action and political action as distinct types of activity subject to different analytical principles. In this respect, one could treat market interaction as governed by alienable property rights while collective action reflects some kind of teleology. This scheme of thought leads to a sequential mode of thinking where market interaction writes the first draft of social life, and with collective action perfecting that first draft. This is the standard analytical scheme of welfare economics, This scheme of thought has analytical simplicity and tractability on its side, This scheme of thought, however, is surely a fictional construction that adheres to the presumptions of benevolent despotism. Yet thus analytical framework is based upon an assumption about knowledge that is fictional and not real.

It is wrong headed to assume that the relevant knowledge for economic activity exists prior to choosing patterns of economic activity. To the contrary, economically relevant knowledge arises in the process of economic action and not prior to it. Collective action occurs conterminously with market action, though we know less about collective action than we know about market processes. Much work remains to be done by way of constructing a theory of democratic political economy where there is no gods-eye view of the phenomena of political economy. To the contrary, that phenomena is continually in the process of being assembled and reassembled, which in turn brings emergent phenomena into the analytical foreground.

References

Aligica, P. D., & Tarko, V. (2012). Polycentricity: From Polanyi to Ostrom, and beyond. *Governance, 25*, 237–252.
Boettke, P. J. (2001). *Calculation and coordination*. London: Routledge.
Boettke, P. J. (2007). Liberty vs. power in economic policy in the 20th and 21st centuries. *Journal of Private Enterprise, 22*, 7–36.
Buchanan, J. M. (1949). The pure theory of public finance: A suggested approach. *Journal of Political Economy, 57*, 496–505.
Buchanan, J. M. (1967). *Public finance in democratic process*. Chapel Hill: University of North Carolina Press.
Buchanan, J. M. (1968). *The demand and supply of public goods*. Chicago: Rand McNally.
Buchanan, J. M., & Tullock, G. (1962). *The calculus of consent*. Ann Arbor: University of Michigan Press.
De Viti de Marco, A. (1888). *Il carattere teorico dell'economia finanziaria*. Rome: Pasqualucci.
De Viti de Marco, A. (1930). *Un trentennio di lotte politiche*. Roma: Collezione Meridionale Editrice.
De Viti de Marco, A. (1936). *First principles of public finance*. London: Jonathan Cape.
Drazen, A. (2002). *Political economy in macroeconomics*. Princeton, NJ: Princeton University Press.
Epstein, R. A. (1995). *Simple rules for a complex world*. Cambridge, MA: Harvard University Press.
Epstein, R. A. (2014). *The Classical Liberal Constitution. Cambridge,* MA: Harvard University Press.

Eusepi, G., & Wagner, R. E. (2013). Tax prices in a democratic polity: The continuing relevance of Antonio de Viti de Marco. *History of Political Economy, 45*, 99–121.
Greve, M. (2012). *The upside-down constitution*. Cambridge, MA: Harvard University Press.
Holcombe, R. G. (2002). *From liberty to democracy: The transformation of american government*. Ann Arbor: University of Michigan Press.
Lindahl, E. (1958 [1919]). Just taxation: A positive solution. In R. A. Musgrave & A. T. Peacock (Eds.), *Classics in the theory of public finance* (pp. 168–176). London: Macmillan.
MacCallum, S. 1970. *The Art of Commuunity*. Menlo Park, CA: Institute for Humane Studies.
Musgrave, R. A. (1939). The voluntary exchange theory of public economy. *Quarterly Journal of Economics, 53*, 213–237.
Ostrom, V. (1987). *The political theory of a compound republic* (2nd ed.). Lincoln: University of Nebraska Press.
Ostrom, V. (1997). *The meaning of democracy and the vulnerability of democracies: A response to Tocqueville's challenge*. Ann Arbor: University of Michigan Press.
Pantaleoni, M. (1911). Considerazioni dulle proprieta di un sistema di prezzi politici. *Giornale degli Economisti, 42*(9–29), 114–133.
Persson, T., & Tabellini, G. (2000). *Political economics: Explaining economic policy*. Cambridge, MA: MIT Press.
Podemska-Mikluch, M., & Wagner, R. E. (2013). Dyads, triads, and the theory of exchange. *Review of Austrian Economics, 26*, 171–182.
Roberts, P. C. (1971). *Alienation and the Soviet Economy*. Albuquerque: University of New Mexico Press.
Samuelson, P. A. (1954). The pure theory of public expenditure. *The Review of Economics and Statistics, 36*, 387–389.
Samuelson, P. A. (1955). Diagrammatic exposition of a theory of public expenditure. *Review of Economics and Statistics, 37*, 350–356.
Schmookler, A. B. (1984). *The parable of the tribes*. Albany: State University of New York Press.
Tanzi, V. (2011). *Government versus markets: The changing economic role of the state*. Cambridge: Cambridge University Press.
Wagner, R. E. (1988). The calculus of consent: A Wicksellian retrospective. *Public Choice, 56*(153), 66.
Wagner, R. E. (2006). Retrogressive regime drift within a theory of emergent order. *Review of Austrian Economics, 19*, 113–123.
Wagner, R. E. (2012). A macro economy as an ecology of plans. *Journal of Economic Behavior and Organization, 82*, 433–444.
Wagner, R. E. (2014). Richard Epstein's Classical Liberal Constitution: A Public Choice Refraction. *New York University Journal of Law and Liberty, 8*, 961–990.
Wagner, R. E. (2017). *James M. Buchanan and liberal political economy: A rational reconstruction*. Lanham, MD: Lexington Books.
Wicksell, K. (1896). *Finanztheoretische untersuchungen*. Jena: Gustav Fischer.
Wicksell, K. (1958). A new principle of just taxation. In R. A. Musgrave & A. T. Peacock (Eds.), *Classics in the theory of public finance* (pp. 72–118). London: Macmillan.

Swimming in a Tuxedo: A Systems Theory Approach to Understanding Politics

David J. Hebert

Abstract This chapter seeks to explain the broad dissatisfaction among the general population of observed political outcomes. To illustrate this, this chapter discusses the growth of the federal tax code over the last century. Despite there being near universal public support for a tax code that is shorter, simpler, and contains fewer loopholes, the precise opposite is provided each year. To explain the disconnect between desires and outcomes, this chapter puts forth a systems theory of politics. Where markets can be thought of as a system driven by competition, politics is best thought of as a system driven by precedent.

Keywords Competition · Markets · Politics · Systems theory

1 Introduction

Suppose that we have a bachelor who is getting dressed in the morning for the day's activities. This bachelor plans on going golfing in the morning, swimming in the afternoon, and to a black-tie dinner in the evening – a busy day, to be sure. With these activities in mind, he dons a pair of golf shoes, a bathing suit and a tuxedo jacket, and sets about his day. Regardless of the quality of any one of these pieces of his outfit, the resulting ensemble would fail spectacularly throughout the day and at all three activities.

While this example is admittedly absurd, it is an apt analogy to characterize the US tax code today, which currently occupies some 70,000 pages.[1] is currently a tool used to accomplish a myriad of different but incongruent tasks. Paul (1997) argues that these incongruencies, and the attempts to resolve them, are a major source of tax code complexity. Consider the following: the consumption of cigarettes is taxed in all 50 states to varying degrees as a means of curbing their consumption due to their negative effects on public health. Producing cigarettes is also subsidized

[1] There is some dispute of this number, with some reporting that the US tax code is roughly 400 pages in length. This disparity comes from

D. J. Hebert (✉)
Aquinas College, Grand Rapids, MI, USA
e-mail: david.hebert@aquinas.edu

D. J. Hebert, D. W. Thomas (eds.), *Emergence, Entanglement, and Political Economy*, Studies in Public Choice 38, https://doi.org/10.1007/978-3-030-56088-1_3

through farm subsidies to tobacco at both the federal and state level both as a general subsidy to farming and specifically as for tobacco. We can also look to the disparate rates at which capital gains and income are taxed, recalling the now-famous example of former Apple, Inc. CEO, Steve Jobs, being paid a salary of a mere $1 per year for his services. Collecting the optimal rate of taxes on a per-person basis as explored in Lindahl (1958) and Mirrless (1976) remains elusive in light of individuals' ability to strategically classify their earnings under different headings which are taxed in different ways.

This chapter seeks to explain political outcomes, and specifically the general public's broad dissatisfaction with them, by using a systems theory approach. Systems theory is the idea that there is a relationship between the whole and its parts. Specifically, each part is interrelated and connected with other, proximate parts. In any system, not only must each individual part perform well but all parts must also work well together. If a part does not perform well or does not work well with the other proximate parts, the system as a whole will perform significantly worse – not just only slightly worse. For example, a car's engine can be thought of as a system. A serpentine belt failure will result in a total and complete failure of the engine, not just a slight reduction in the operability of the engine, even if the rest of the engine is of extraordinarily high quality.

Systems are everywhere. There are biological, ecological, and environmental systems some of which are purportedly in dire need of attention lest we cause irrevocable harm. Economists also make plenty of references to systems. We have various retirement systems, the tax system, and the budget system, to name just a few. More broadly, we have political systems, market systems, and cultural systems. We even treat "system" as an adjective in some cases as is the case with systemic bias. Despite this word's wide usage, very few economists take seriously the notion of systems theory and how it applies to understanding the world in which we live, instead opting to resort to some form of a representative agent type model. One economist who does not suffer such a shortcoming is Richard Wagner in Politics as a Peculiar Business (Wagner 2016).

While Wagner uses systems theory in his work, he highlights residual claimancy and issues of scalability as potential areas of tension. This chapter takes a different tack and instead explains the wide divergence in the satisfaction of outcomes in markets and politics as a result of the interchangeability of parts of the systems. In doing so, this chapter does not so much correct a problem in Wagner (2016), but rather extends it. Markets are characterized by dynamic changes through time while politics is characterized by slow-moving changes. Some degree of this slow-moving pace of change in politics may have been intentional in the founding of the federal system of government Hebert (forthcoming).

Both markets and politics, as realms of activity, can be thought of as systems with many parts that must interact with one another to produce any whole. Leonard Read highlights the systemic qualities of the market by exploring each of the parts that constitutes the whole of making a pencil (Read 1996) Likewise, Smith (1776) does the same with the story of a wool coat. While these are systems with specific ends in mind, systems can also been used to explain broader topics. For example,

Paris gets fed (Bastiat 1964). In each of these systems, many parts must interact in such a way as to produce the whole that is the outcome.

Political outcomes can also be thought of in this same systems theory approach. Any law that passes will be the result of not just one person's mind, but instead is brought about in a quasi-market like process as explored in Hebert and Wagner (2013) and Hebert (2016). With the U.S. tax code as an example, we can think of the House Ways and Means Committee, the Joint Committee on Taxation, the Joint Economic Committee, the House and Senate Committees on the Budget, both the House of Representatives as a whole and the Senate as a whole, and the President all as individual parts that must work in concert together to create and pass any tax bill. Moreover, introducing time into this equation and noting that the federal tax code, which today is made up of some 70,000 pages of text and definitions, is the result of this same system operating over several periods makes this system even more complicated to envision, but not imagine.

The difference between these two types of systems, markets and politics, that this highlights is the ease with which parts can be substituted and the processes by which those parts are substituted. In markets, the process of substituting one part for another is relatively simple and commonplace. An automotive company is free to purchase its steel, for example, from any steel producing company it wishes and can thereby choose along dimensions of e.g. price and quality. In politics, however, individual parts cannot be as easily substituted as each bill is assigned to the committees which have legislative jurisdiction over particular topics. Some committees have very broad jurisdiction (e.g. the House Ways and Means Committee) while others have comparatively narrower jurisdiction (e.g. the Joint Committee on Printing, which oversees the Government Publishing Office). In either case, any bill will be assigned in lockstep to certain committees and must go through these committees before going before the full chamber. Important in this is the notion of committee jurisdiction. As highlighted in Shepsle and Weingast (1987) and Martin and Thomas (2013), committees have unique, non-overlapping jurisdictions over legislative areas. They do not, however, have ipso facto jurisdictions over particular proposals, which may touch on several legislative areas. A proposal may be put forth, for example, that deals with taxing cigarettes as a means of improving health outcomes. This proposal would fall under the legislative jurisdiction of committees pertaining to both health and taxes, with the Chamber's Parliamentarian and Majority Leader ultimately deciding the legislative path that this proposal would have to travel before reaching the Chamber's floor for a full vote.

The rest of this chapter will be organized as follows: Sections 2 and 3 provides an explanation of why parts must exist. Section 3 provides a systems theory approach to understanding markets and politics, paying particular attention to the case of the federal government in the United States.[2] Section 4 compares and contrasts the behavior of parts within markets and politics. Section 5 provides concluding remarks.

[2]This is not due to some special status of the U.S. federal government – it is simply the institution with which I am most familiar. The insights here apply with equal force, though with slight alteration to the particulars, to any governmental system.

2 Why Parts?

As a first step toward explaining a systems theory approach to anything, we must recognize the existence of parts. Economists have a ready answer for the existence of parts within market settings found in the related concepts of comparative advantage, specialization, and mutually beneficial exchange. Not even One Big Cartel, as Rothbard (2009) refers to, is able to exist for much the same reasons as highlighted in Hayek (1937, 1945) – economic calculation. Economic calculation depends vitally on the existence of market prices, which can only be generated in market settings that are external to the Cartel. As Rothbard (2009) says, "When any of these external markets disappears, because all are absorbed within the province of a single firm, calculability disappears, and there is no way for the firm rationally to allocate factors to that specific area. The more these limits are encroached upon, the greater and greater will be the sphere of irrationality, and the more difficult it will be to avoid losses. One big cartel would not be able rationally to allocate producers' goods at all and hence could not avoid severe losses. Consequently, it could never really be established, and, if tried, would quickly break asunder."

But why have parts in a parliamentary assembly such as the U.S. Congress? After all, if the argument advanced in this chapter is that the political system and the existence of its constituent parts at least contributes to the existing problems observed today, it would seem like an easy solution would be to reduce the system to one part known as "the whole." The reason for parts can be found in de Jouvenal (1961).

Imagine as a start that we have a legislative body that has no committees. For simplicity, we will assume that this legislative body is comprised of 100 individual members. First of all, absent a framework for making decisions, this group is nothing short of a mob (Brennan and Buchanan 2000; Congleton 2011). Let's suppose that a simple majority rule is used and that, prior to the vote, everyone in the assembly is afforded 5 min of speaking time to discuss the proposal. Under this rule, the meeting would be 8 h and 20 min long. This is problematic for two reasons. First, a meeting of this length is wholly untenable and it is virtually impossible for any person to reasonably be expected to pay attention for this amount of time. Second, 5 min is nowhere near enough time for a person to be able to articulate their position in any sort of a meaningful way. Thus, this legislative body would end up with a meeting of an untenable length where little of substance was said. Should the chair of the meeting wish to make the meeting short enough to be tenable while still affording everyone equal speaking time, they would have to reduce the amount of time each person was allotted even further, which would only make each person's remarks all the less meaningful. If, instead, the chair wished to give everyone more time to speak so that they could make a proper argument, the meeting time would balloon into days on end, which would be untenable both from a logistical standpoint and from the perspective of the participants, who must not only remember each argument that they heard but also digest and assess each argument as well.

This also ignores the time-cost of actually reading the bills and any other relevant materials. Hebert and Wagner (2013) introduces some rough calculations on the length of time it would take to read a bill as well as the expert testimonies that typically accompany such bills, finding that each bill would require about 11 h of reading.[3] As the authors note that while this is a large amount of reading for one bill, it is not insurmountable. However, in 2013, there were 6677 bills introduced to Congress of which 861 ultimately passed. To be sure, not all bills will require 11 h of reading (some of the bills are certainly perfunctory and require little to no reading), but still, we can easily imagine even a staff of 20 people having a hard time keeping up with the sheer volume of reading required to cast an informed vote on each and every proposal.

A committee system can, in theory, resolve all of these issues.[4] It reduces the number of people who are able to speak on a particular bill, which means that each person can speak for a longer amount of time without causing the meeting's length to balloon out of control. It also reduces the amount of reading necessary for each member of Congress to the bills over which they have jurisdiction.[5] Finally, it allows the members of the committee to develop some degree of expertise in particular areas of policy such that they have more meaningful insights to offer on particular proposals and issues.

In many ways, the existence of parts in the political sphere mirrors the existence of parts in the market sphere. In theory, both have their roots in the benefits to the whole of specialization among the parts. Rather than task each person with doing everything for themselves or some fraction of everything for the benefit of the whole, each person is tasked with a specific step of a production process and specializes in doing that one particular step. Further, each part interacts with other proximate parts in a specific way and only indirectly with other, more distant parts. As above, the Sri Lankan graphite miners do not interact directly with the loggers in California but are nonetheless connected. Likewise, the House Ways & Means Committee does not interact directly with the Senate Budget Committee, but the two are still likewise connected through the workings of Congress.

Despite this, having a system of parts rather than One Big Part do all the work does have its downsides. While having specialized parts working together drastically increases the potential for output of any system, it also increases the difficulty of trying to assign blame when a system does not operate properly. Consider a Volkswagen Tiguan that, initially, operates without any trouble and is quite pleasant. After some time, however, this car can no longer start and that the same problem arises in a large fraction of Volkswagen Tiguans. First, it is very likely that Volkswagen will accept responsibility for this and offer some sort of recall/repair program at no charge to the owner. Second, Volkswagen will begin work on figuring

[3] This assumes an average reading speed of about 250 words per minute, 60 pages for the bill, and five to seven, 30 page expert testimonies

[4] Though Hebert (2018) and Hebert and Wagner (2018) argue that there may be cause for concern with the real-world implementation of this theoretical solution.

[5] Though this can also be detrimental, with Nancy Pelosi's famous remark of "we have to pass the bill so that you can find out what is in it" referring to the Affordable Care Act in 2010 highlights this.

out what is causing the problem. A car not starting can be caused by a failure in a litany of different components; perhaps the starter motor is broken or maybe the engine is somehow seized. Regardless, Volkswagen will undertake the costly activity of figuring out what is going wrong and come up with a solution. Going forward, they may choose to work with a different vendor when purchasing e.g. their starter motors, switching from perhaps Duralast to Valeo. In this case, Volkswagen would be substituting a different part in their production process to produce the whole that is the Volkswagen Tiguan. What should be clear is that in the case of market participants, blame can be assigned and changes can be made to address any potential problems.

In the political setting, however, this is not as easily done. In the case of the United States, the federal tax code occupies some 70,000 pages. When asked, only 16% of Americans view the current tax code as "fair."

This should seem a bit odd since all legislation requires at least a simple majority to pass. To be sure, in a representative democracy, it is easy to see how less than a majority of voters can support an issue that nonetheless gets a majority of representatives' votes (see Buchanan and Tullock (1962, Appendix A)) but such a wide disparity is slightly harder to imagine. While at a superficial level, it is easy to blame Congress for passing such a tax code, difficulties arise in figuring out which part, exactly, is to blame for the observed outcome. This is in part because of what Wagner (2016) refers to as the "shell game" of politics where the analytical focus is placed on the outcome without digging deeper into the workings of the system. This leads, as Podemska-Mikluch (2014) discusses, to asking the wrong questions about the nature of the problem. With the wrong questions being asked, there is little to no hope of a truly corrective answer being given. The proceeding section highlights what would be necessary to ask the correct type of questions.

3 Markets and Politics as Systems

At a surface level, it is relatively straight-forward to imagine a market as a system, even though this is often neglected. Adam Ferguson's (1767) famous remark that "nations stumble upon establishments, which are indeed the result of human action but not the execution of any human design" and Hayek's descriptions of spontaneous orders can be thought of in terms of systems theory.

We can think broadly, as Wagner (2016) does, of society as consisting of two levels: an action level and a system level.[6] At the action level are the individual people who perform tasks. It is at this level where action takes place, as the individual parts of a system perform actions. At the system level are the observed

[6] Wagner distinguishes between robotic and creative systems, where a robotic system would describe individual mechanical parts that perform a task but do not actively choose (e.g. a coffee maker) where a creative system is characterized by parts that do choose (e.g. people). This chapter is concerned only with creative systems.

outcomes of the actions and interactions of the people/parts. Here, no action takes place as it is simply the result of the actions that took place at the action level. By way of example, we can think of traffic patterns along a highway that is congested. At the action level are the individual people who are driving their cars down a highway, each acting and interacting in various ways. At the systems level, if there are too many cars on the highway, we would observe a traffic jam, whereby some of the cars must slow down briefly in order to avoid collision and can then speed up once traffic clears. Looking down on this traffic pattern from the sky, we might see a traffic jam that grows and shrinks. Obviously, there is no such entity as a "traffic jam" that is growing or shrinking, but rather this appearance is the result of the individual drivers driving down the road and interacting with one another. As another example that Wagner likes to use, we can think of a game of billiards (see, for example, Wagner (2012, pg 24–25)). The action level is the player moving the cue stick in such a way as to strike the cue ball into the object ball whereas the systems level is the dispersion of the various non-object balls around the rest of the table as a result of the cue ball striking the object ball.

We can apply this same insight to the production of any product. Looking at Read (1996) we can see that there are many individual parts that comprise the system that produces a pencil. There is the logging company in Northern California and Oregon which must fell the cedar trees of straight grain and the trucking company that produced the trucks that carried the cedar logs to the mill in San Leandro, California. Later in the process, graphite from Sri Lanka, clay from Mississippi, and candelilla from Mexico are all combined to make the leads that go into the pencil. And so on, ad (virtually-) infinitum. Read concludes his essay by noting "the absence of a master mind, of anyone dictating of forcibly directing these countless actions which bring [a pencil] into being." Read is correct. The pencil is a result of a system that produces pencils, but the system itself was not designed by any one person nor is it actively coordinated by any one person or any group of persons.

Systems can, and do, evolve over time. There is little doubt that some logging companies have vertically integrated with, for example, lumber mills and that now the system which produces a pencil might be in some sense smaller than it was back in 1958 when Leonard Read first wrote his essay. Alternatively, it might be larger as companies divide along lines of specialization.

New parts can also rise and established parts can whither, harking back to Schumpeter's insights of creative destruction. Despite this, this change to the system did not occur as a top-down command by some coordinator of the system. Instead, it emerged from the bottom-up as individual parts merge, split, or morph into new parts that were previously unimagined.

It is also important to recognize that not every part of a system is directly connected to every other part of a system, which reflects the idea that knowledge is dispersed among society (Hayek 1937, 1945). The miners in Sri Lanka do not directly interact with, for example, the loggers in California, but their actions do affect and are affected by one another. For example, a forest fire in California which destroys a large amount of cedar trees would cause an increase in the price of lumber. This would cause the pencil-making company to produce fewer pencils, which in turn would lead them to purchase less graphite from the Sri Lankan miners. In today's world of increasingly available information and news coverage, the miners in Sri Lanka may become aware of the forest fire in California through watching the evening news or reading a world news report, but the exact effect (if any) that this would have on them would still remain unclear. In any event, the effect of such an external force on one node or part of a system would cause, through the workings of the system, changes in the behaviors of other, more distant nodes.

Like markets, we can also think of politics as a form of system. Hebert and Wagner (2013) does this, albeit without describing itself as a systems theory approach to tax policy. There, the authors describe the process by which a well-intentioned politician would have to complete in order to affect a change in the federal tax code. First, this politician would almost certainly need to have a seat on the House Ways and Means Committee, as Article 1, Section 7, Clause 1 of the U.S. Constitution (often referred to as the Origination Clause) states that all bills for raising revenue must originate in the House. The House Ways and Means Committee was first established as a standing committee in 1795[7] and was given explicit jurisdiction over taxes and spending, the latter of which was separated and given to the newly created Appropriations Committee in 1865 (Kennon and Rogers 1991). This committee is comprised of six subcommittees (Health, Worker and Family Support, Oversight, Select Revenue Measures, Social Security, and Trade), each of which has jurisdiction over tax policy pertaining to those areas. In cases where jurisdiction is not clear, the Chair of the committee can ultimately decide which subcommittee has jurisdiction. As is often the case, however, a proposed tax bill may affect areas of policy that fall within multiple subcommittees. In these cases, each subcommittee is given jurisdiction over writing the relevant parts of the proposal, which are then stitched together in much the same way (as Hebert and Wagner (2013) describes) that Frankenstein's monster is stitched together.

The above outlines the systematic qualities of just one committee involved in passing a hypothetical, very narrow bill on "taxes." Even in this case, it is clear that systems are at play. In the real world, proposed bills are not so simple and many different committees may have a legitimate jurisdictional claim to a bill. Despite this, a proposed bill would be referred to a single committee for consideration and mark-up. This changed in 1975 and again in 1995, when the rules of the House were changed. As a result of these two rule changes, any piece of legislation may now be sent to multiple committees, with the caveat that if legislation is referred to multiple committees, it must either be considered in its entirety by one committee at a time (in a process known as sequential referral) or the legislation may be split into multiple parts, each of which can be considered by one committee at a time (a process known as split referral).

Thus, when deciding where to refer proposed legislation, the Speaker of the House has three options: (1) refer it to a single committee and only to that committee,

[7]Though a Ways and Means Committee was established in the First Congress in 1789, it was disbanded after a mere 8 weeks

(2) refer it sequentially to more than one committee, or (3) split the proposed legislation into multiple parts and refer it to multiple committees simultaneously. Because of the tremendous power that this creates, the Office of the Parliamentarian (which was created under Article 1, Section 5 of the Constitution) is charged with advising presiding officers, members, and staff of procedural questions as well as historical precedent. The principle of stare decisis is held to by the Speaker, with the parliamentarian providing clarification on earlier and pertinent precedents. While there are no formal rules that require the Speaker to abide by the advice and counsel of the parliamentarian, both the House and the Senate have strong informal rules that make deviations from the parliamentarian's counsel exceedingly rare which is more commonly known as the deference norm (Martin and Thomas 2011).

A key insight here is that once the Speaker of the House (in consultation with the House Parliamentarian) has decided the referral path, the system that will ultimately produce the bill is, for all intents and purposes, set. The only way for this referral path to be changed is for the bill itself to be entirely withdrawn, a new proposal written, and re-submitted to the Speaker for new consideration. Even if this were to happen, the bill would, through the principle of stare decisis, be very likely to receive the same referral path. A clever politician who is familiar with past precedent for bills might seek to craft a bill in such a way as to influence the Speaker's referral decision. They might also, through bargaining with the Speaker, try to influence whether their bill is referred sequentially or split into multiple parts, but the amount of influence that any individual politician can wield in this situation is limited, again due to the office of the Parliamentarian and the strict observed principle of stare decisis and the deference norm.

What should be clear is that, while both markets and politics are comprised of systems, these systems operate under different rules. In the market setting, it is very much a system driven by competition. In politics, however, this system is driven by precedent. This difference is what causes the large disparity in the satisfaction between markets and politics.

4 The Behavior of Parts

Markets and politics share more in common than is often recognized. They are both comprised of individual people operating within a framework of rules who are all striving to do the best that they can to advance whatever interests they have. And as Wagner (2016) argues, "political enterprises must attract supporters just as must commercial enterprises."

In markets, any single part of a system can be replaced at any time if it is not performing well enough by the standards of some other party, whether they be a part of that system or not. As the common phrase goes, "build a better mousetrap, and the world will beat a path to your door." While not typically thought of in these terms, this insight can be taken to mean that any part which does not add sufficient value relative to its cost will be discarded in favor of another, comparable part.

Further, this quest to change parts of a system for better parts marches on; if a better part exists (or if a system as a whole can be changed in some way for the better), entrepreneurs will find it.

This puts tremendous pressures on any existing market enterprise. In order to continue, each must be constantly evaluating its processes of production, searching tirelessly for even the smallest of margins upon which to improve. The successes and failures of these endeavors are communicated through profits and losses. Successfully providing sufficient value relative to cost is evidenced through the earning of profit. Examples of this abound: Amazon has completely revolutionized the shipping industry. Netflix fundamentally changed the way that video media is delivered to consumers. Companies like Uber and Lyft have dramatically changed personal transportation. Failure to provide sufficient value relative to cost (and to find such margins for improvement) will eventually result in the demise of that enterprise, which is experienced as losses for its owners and workers. Notable examples of this include Blockbuster, Toys "R" Us, and Radio Shack, each of which failed to keep up with changing technologies and consumer preferences.

Contrast this with congressional committees. In the House alone, there are 23 standing committees and 802 total committee assignments.[8] Each of these committees is given jurisdiction over bills pertaining to particular topics. Thus, if a proposed bill would affect, e.g. national parks, it would go before the U.S. Senate Energy and Natural Resources Committee, and specifically it is subcommittee on National Parks in the Senate and the Natural Resources Committee in the House of Representatives. Unlike their market enterprise counterparts, these political enterprises cannot be substituted. If a Congressperson or voter is unhappy, for whatever reason, with the bills that come out of a particular committee, there is no means by which that committee could be substituted with another, more effective committee. In other words: there is no competition among parts within Congress.

Despite the potential pitfalls here, there are benefits to this type of arrangement. Chiefly, having this requirement prevents any one individual member from exercising too broad of power. However, each member of a committee wields significant specific power in the sense that any bill that falls within the jurisdiction of their committee will almost certainly be considered by that committee prior to being brought to the floor of the chamber for consideration. In the event that the bill somehow bypasses the committee stage, a point of order can be raised which would refer the bill to the committee. Having this power of consideration is what gives rise to the "political bazaar" that Wagner (2016, pg. 163) refers to, where "members of parliament are engaged in putting together legislative deals that will attain concurrence among the relevant set of parliamentary members, starting with the relevant committee and then extending to the full assembly." Individual politicians must have something of value that they can bring to the exchange. While their support through a vote in the affirmative is certainly necessary, it is insufficient absent the ability to write that which will be voted on to begin with.

[8]These figures do not include Joint committees

Another area where market parts and political parts differ can be found in the discussion of the water-diamond paradox and the importance of marginal analysis. In market settings, it can be said that "the automotive industry" is beholden to "the steel industry" for the production of car frames. To say so, however, is to commit the same fallacy as the water-diamond paradox that puzzled economists up until the marginal revolution. In this example, notions of the automotive industry and the steel industry are an oversimplification, as there are many participants in the automotive and steel industries. Each participant is constantly competing against one another for business. So while on the surface, it is true that the automotive industry could not exist without the steel industry, no participant of either industry is beholden to any participant in the other industry. General Motors is free to purchase steel from ArcelorMittal, China Baowu Steel Group, Nippon Steel & Sumimoto Metal, Sabre Steel, Inc., Eagle National Steel, or Beartech Alloys, Inc., to name just a few steel companies. Likewise, these steel companies are free to sell their steel to General Motors, Ford Motor Company, Chrysler, Honda, Toyota, Hyundai, and a litany of other automotive companies (and other, non-automotive companies). As such, no one company in either industry is beholden to any one company in the other industry.

However, in the political arena, there is a much greater degree of beholdenness to parts. Any bill that deals with taxation must, per the Constitution, originate in the House Ways & Means Committee. If the bill is going to entail spending, it must go through the Appropriations Committee and its relevant subcommittee and most likely the Budget committee of each chamber. If it has to do with anything affecting the financial services industry, the bill must go through each chamber's Finance committee. Further, the person drafting the legislation has no control over the system that will ultimately produce the bill as the committee assignment process is entirely decided by the Speaker of the House and the Parliamentarian. Because of this, the incentive of any individual politician is to gain a seat on the most powerful committee that they can. In the case of the U.S. House of Representatives, these committees are typically recognized as being the Appropriations, Rules, Ways & Means, Energy & Commerce, and Financial Services committees.

Hebert and Wagner (2018) discusses how political parties themselves are interest groups and not mere disseminators of information to the general public, as modeled in Denzau and Munger (1986) and Mueller and Stratmann (1994) or clearinghouses for vote-trading activities (Stratmann 1992). Rather, political parties have their own interests and act not as passive or neutral intermediaries between voters and politicians but instead shape the discussion around particular topics in such a way as to achieve the party's goals and the goals of the individual party members. Likewise, Hebert (2018) graphically demonstrates how control over selection of committee members can and does influence the final outcome of a proposed piece of legislation.

Combining these insights, the incentive of any particular politician are not necessarily in line with the wishes of their constituency. It may be, but importantly, it also may not be.[9] Instead, their incentive is to sufficiently appease the group in charge of assigning committee seats such that they can gain a seat on the above-mentioned committees. Once there, however, they must continue to appease the Speaker of the House and a select few other party members lest they be removed from a committee.

Thus, the incentive of any individual part of the system that produces legislation is not necessarily to work well with other, proximate parts, but instead to do what the Party wishes them to do. This creates a lack of coherence among the parts within the legislative system, stymieing production. As discussed in Hebert (2019) this is actually a feature of the legislative process and not a bug: "the underlying principle guiding the original writing of the Constitution was one of caution. It was not designed to empower good people or to enable 'good' to be done, but rather to provide numerous means through which a small number of politicians could prevent a bill from becoming law." Today, however, government activity comprises some 40% of all economic activity in the US. Because of this, what government does has a real and discernible effect on the day-to-day lives of citizens. With a system explicitly designed to be unproductive being comprised of parts that cannot be substituted and operated by people whose incentives are not guaranteed to be in-line with the desires of the citizens themselves, an unproductive and unsatisfactory outcome can be the only result.

5 Conclusion

Viewing markets as systems is an analogy commonly used among economists. Despite this, few economists actually engage in systems theory, instead opting to collapse an entire system into some sort of a representative agent model. While this is not wholly useless, it does render some important questions unanswerable and perhaps even unasked. Applying systems theory to the realm of politics and using the tools of economics is a relatively unexplored area. This chapter seeks to rectify this.

This chapter began with the analogy of a bachelor wearing golf shoes, a bathing suit, and a tuxedo jacket and noted that the resulting ensemble would fail spectacularly throughout each of the day's activities. With the increased scope (and scale) of the tasks that have been assigned to government, this illustration accurately characterizes the current state of government today. With the individual parts all acting independently and not in concert with other, proximate parts, the full ensemble loses the ability to be effective at anything. This is different from the knowledge-problem identified by Austrian economists and also different from the incentive-problem as it is typically extolled by public choice economists. Instead, this new

[9] Further, Hebert and Wagner (2018) discusses how even well-informed constituents could end up supporting measures that are actually counter to their own wishes.

problem is a systemic one, which provides a starting point for new questions and explanations into problems in political economy.

References

Bastiat, F. (1964). *Economic harmonies*. Irvington-on-Hudson, NY: Foundation for Economic Education.

Brennan, G., & Buchanan, J. (2000). *The reason of rules: Constitutional political economy*. Indianapolis, IN: Liberty Fund.

Buchanan, J., & Tullock, G. (1962). *The Calculus of consent: Logical foundations of constitutional democracy*. Indianapolis, IN: Liberty Fund.

Congleton, R. (2011). *Perfecting parliament: Constitutional reform liberalism, and the rise of Western democracy*. Cambridge, UK: Cambridge University Press.

de Jouvenal, B. (1961). Seminar exercise: The Chairman's problem. *The American Political Science Review, 55*, 367–372.

Denzau, A., & Munger, M. (1986). Legislators and interest groups: How unorganized interests get represented. *The American Political Science Review, 80*, 89–106.

Ferguson, A. (1767). Essay on the history of civil society.

Hayek, F. (1937). Economics and knowledge. *Economica, 4*, 33–54.

Hayek, F. (1945). The use of knowledge in society. *American Economic Review, 35*, 519–530.

Hebert, D. (2016). Micro-level Catallactic public finance. *Journal of Public Finance and Public Choice, 32*, 123–148.

Hebert, D. (2018). The Spontaneous Order of Politics. In Steven Horwitz (Ed.), A*ustrian Economics: The Next Generation*. Advances in Austrian Economics, Vol. 23. Emerald Publishing Limited. Pg. 131–144.

Hebert, D. (2019). The Chairman's solution. *The Journal of Public Finance and Public Choice, 34*, 71–82.

Hebert, D. (forthcoming). Why deficits? In J. Merrifield, B. Poulson, & R. Wagner (Eds.), *The U.S. debt crisis: New perspectives*. Washington, DC: Cato Institute.

Hebert, D., & Wagner, R. E. (2013). Taxation as a quasi-market process: Explanation, exhortation, and the choice of analytical windows. *Journal of Public Finance and Public Choice, 31*, 163–177.

Hebert, D., & Wagner, R. (2018). Political parties: Insights from a tri-planar model of political economy. *Constitutional Political Economy, 29*, 253–267.

Kennon, R., & Rogers, R. (1991). *The committee on ways and means: A bicentennial history, 1789–1989*. Washington, DC: GPO.

Lindahl, E. (1958). Just taxation – A positive solution. In Musgrave & Peacock (Eds.), *Classics in the theory of public finance* (pp. 168–176). St. Martin's Press.

Martin, A., & Thomas, D. (2011). Two-tiered political entrepreneurship and the congressional committee system. *Public Choice, 154*, 21–37.

Martin, A., & Thomas, D. (2013). Two-tiered entrepreneurship and the congressional committee system. *Public Choice, 154*, 21–37.

Mirrless, J. (1976). Optimal tax theory: A synthesis. *Journal of Public Economics, 6*, 327–358.

Mueller, D., & Stratmann, T. (1994). Informative and persuasive campaigning. *Public Choice, 81*, 55–77.

Paul, D. (1997). The Sources of Tax Complexity: How Much Simplicity Can Fundamental Tax Reform Achieve? *The North Carolina Law Review, 76*, 151–220..

Podemska-Mikluch, M. (2014). Public policy: Object of choice or emergent phenomena? Learning from the implementation of the medical reimbursement act in Poland. *Advances in Austrian Economics, 18*, 93–110.

Read, L. (1996). *I, pencil: My family tree as told to Leonard Read*. Irvington-on-Hudson, NY: Pamphlet, Foundation for Economic Education.
Rothbard, M. (2009). *Man, economy, and state*. Auburn, AL: Ludwig von Mises Institute.
Smith, A. (1776). *An inquiry into the nature and causes of the wealth of nations*. Indianapolis, IN: Liberty Fund.
Shepsle, K., & Weingast, B. (1987). The institutional foundations of committee power. *The American Political Science Review, 81*(1), 85–104.
Stratmann, T. (1992). The effects of logrolling on congressional voting. *American Economic Review, 82*, 1162–1176.
Wagner, R. E. (2012). *Deficits, debt, and democracy: Wrestling with tragedy on the fiscal commons*. Northampton, MA: Edward Elgar Publishing.
Wagner, R. E. (2016). *Politics as a peculiar business: Insights from a theory of entangled political economy*. Northampton, MA: Edward Elgar Publishing.

Complex and Entangled Public Policy: Here Be Dragons

Abigail Devereaux

Abstract The tools and concepts of the emerging field of complexity science—like agent-based modeling, network theory, and machine learning—can offer powerful insights to economists and crafters of public policy. Complexity science enables us to explicitly model relationships between individuals and institutions, asymmetric information and influence, the emergence of unplanned emergent social orders, and dynamically adaptive individuals. In the last few decades the tools of complexity science have been applied to the problem of public goods provision, correcting hypothesized behavioral biases, and raising the efficiency of policy implementation. These analyses often lack public choice perspectives, which may complicate and even obviate their findings when the designer becomes entangled with the complex structures in his models. Furthermore, there remains a good deal of work to be done to harmonize traditional public choice work with the tools and insights of complexity science. Uncharted waters must eventually be charted; we hope to begin in such a way that avoids the worst of the dragons.

Keywords Complexity economics · Public choice · Entangled political economy · Machine learning · Agent-based modeling

JEL Codes H40 · H50 · P41 · P48 · P50

1 Introduction

> In our hour of greatest need, societies around the world are left to grope in the dark without a theory. That, to us, is a systemic failure of the economics profession. (Colander et al. 2014).

In the wake of the 2007–8 financial crisis, there arose another crisis: a crisis in confidence about the methodological underpinnings of modern macroeconomics, namely, the theory of dynamic stochastic general equilibrium (DSGE)

A. Devereaux (✉)
Wichita State University, Wichita, KS, USA

D. J. Hebert, D. W. Thomas (eds.), *Emergence, Entanglement, and Political Economy*, Studies in Public Choice 38, https://doi.org/10.1007/978-3-030-56088-1_4

(Romer 2016; Stiglitz 2018). The theory of DSGE is simplistic to be analytically tractable, and the models used for policy-making (by, say, the Federal Reserve) are further stripped of most of their economic realism. In the aftermath of the financial crisis, complexity economists argued that equilibrium theorizing in general cannot explain phenomena crucial to understanding booms and busts, like heterogeneous expectations, cascades, herding effects, and phase transitions (Helbing and Kirman 2013; Farmer and Foley 2009).

The 2007–2008 financial crisis also led some complexity economists to make policy statements, some broad and focused on the fundamental relationship between experts and the economy, and others, more detailed. Brian Arthur, one of the fathers of complexity economics, stated that

> …complexity teaches us that markets left to themselves possess a tendency to bubbles and crashes, induce a multiplicity of local attractor states, propagate events through financial networks, and generate a sequence of technological solutions and challenges, and this opens a role for policies of regulating excess, nudging towards favored outcomes, and judiciously fostering conditions for innovation. (Arthur 2014: 23-4).

The message sent by complexity economists post-crisis is clear: it is no longer enough to theorize about crises in terms of dampened harmonic oscillator models, indicators and shocks. But how true is the claim that the turbulent nature of markets is due largely to (1) "markets left to themselves," and that turbulence implies (2) "policies of regulating excess," (3) "nudging towards favored outcomes," and (4) "fostering conditions for innovation"?

Complexity science enables us to explicitly model relationships between individuals and institutions, asymmetric information and influence, the emergence of unplanned emergent social orders, and dynamically adaptive individuals using the many and myriad tools of complexity theorizing like graph theory, game theory, systems theory, agent-based modeling, machine learning on massive data sets, and algorithms that guide or automatize decision-making. With these tools, complexity economists hope to explicitly model economic phenomena that feature dynamically adaptive individuals, the emergence of unplanned social orders, the relationships and feedbacks between individuals and social orders, asymmetric information and influence, bounded rationality and choice using fast-and-frugal heuristics, and open-ended evolution and growth.

As a complexity economist, part of my contribution to this conversation is to bring the designer into his design, to remind ourselves that public governance through the use of artificial intelligence (AI), algorithmic decision-making and guidance, machine learning, and computational simulations must acknowledge entangled political economy (Wagner 2016; Novak 2018). Entangled political economy explicitly recognizes the difference between how agents make plans and what they perceive it is possible to do as the system evolves; possibilities are a function of not just the will of system agents, but the joint activities of many special interest groups and how those groups interact with the system's predominant mode of governance (Hebert and Wagner 2018). Experts can change how other agents in the system plan, and what they believe it is possible to do, through the very act of intervening on the system; experts are themselves entangled with their design, and with the agents they intervene upon (Koppl 2018).

The paper is organized as follows: Section 2 gives a short history of the development of complexity economics, to prime the mind for the following sections. Section 3 introduces the cutting-edge tools of complexity economics, and how these tools are being used to make policy. Section 4 is about dragons. Section 5 concludes.

2 The Development of Complexity Economics: A Short History

Complexity in economics has a turbulent history befit its subject matter. In the age of Adam Smith, complexity was the paradigm. In his Theory of Moral Sentiments, Smith made much of how the rubric-happy casuists of the Catholic church were not able to develop a code of all sinful situations and their rectification due to the innumerable significant subtleties that can shape any given situation and its solution (Smith 2010 (1752)). Thus, the business of saving someone's soul was not programmable.

In the early twentieth century, a great shift occurred from economists treating their subject as a study of heterogeneous entrepreneurs, intricate webs of trade and factions, and complicated industries with detailed and specific constraints and challenges, to the physics of a ball rolling over bumpy terrain. Despite warnings from Thorstein Veblen (1898: Ch 16) and Knut Wicksell (1898: xxx) about the limited scope of using Newtonian physics to model important areas of economic analysis, it took less than 40 years for analytically tractable rational agents and static system-level equilibria to envelop mainstream economic theory.

In the mid-twentieth century, economics became a science focused on short-term control, punctuated by the frequent discovery of puzzles unsolvable by idealized "market" models. Throughout the mid-century, economists continued to trade explanatory power for mathematical convenience, until theorists like Lewis (1985) and Shafer and Sonneschein (1982) cast doubt on the core of economic theory's power, its purported generality and applicability. Alain Lewis, Kenneth Arrow's protégé, proved that excess demands were incomputable. This means that optimizing individual equilibria, then using representative optimizing agents to microfound macroeconomics, predicts the existence of social optima that may or may not be computationally realizable by individuals, markets, or policy-makers.

That is, Lewis discovered that attaining predicted neoclassical equilibria is generally implausible and may be impossible by any conceivable system of individual and public choice.

In response to Sonneschein-Mantel-Debreu, economic methodology fractured somewhat away from equilibrium theorizing, though these theories remain the foundation upon which new scholars are trained (Rizvi 2006; Kirman 2004).

Mechanism design theory—and its subfields computable general equilibrium theory and algorithmic game theory—invoke approximation as a way saving the infrastructure of fixed-point economic theory. Sadly, there is no known approximate method for finding fixed points that can meaningfully parallel utility and profit optima and thus avoid the issues discovered by the SMD theorem and by Lewis (1985) (Velupillai 2008, 2016).

If excess demands are incomputable, then algorithmic and mechanistic searches for ways to nudge systems from suboptimal to more-optimal outcomes must have provably computable goals in mind. It is insufficient to prove there is a market failure in the traditional manner of neoclassical existence proofs and then conduct a programmatical policy to alter the system to more resemble the neoclassical optimal state, because we have not yet proved that the neoclassical goals are welfare-optimal in a computable system.

At the same time control theorists were grappling with the implications of Sonneschein-Mantel-Debreu and Lewis's exposition of the noncomputability of excess demands, bounded rationality theorists were laying the foundations for complexity economics as defined by Brian Arthur (2014) and others (Gallegati and Kirman 2012). Social scientists unconstrained by axiom systems yet pressured by the exigencies of the Cold War conceived of different kinds of human behavior that were neoclassically rational at the individual level but systemically irrational, and vice-versa (see in particular Simon 1972 and Schelling 1978). Experiments showed that real decisions were in many ways not neoclassically rational (Smith 2003). Theorists of radical subjectivism warned of mistaking macroeconomics for microeconomics, and vice-versa (Shackle 1972; Lachmann 1976).

Regardless of these discoveries, modern macroeconomics utilized for the purposes of policymaking has been expressed in terms of equilibrium theorizing (Romer 2016). Evidence has continued to accrue since Lewis's demonstration that is computationally hard or close to it for even moderately complicated individuals and economies to attain a unique equilibrium (Papadimitriou 1994; Velupillai 2007; Babichenko and Rubinstein 2016). Unfortunately for the economy, it took the global financial crisis of 2007–2008 to make many (though not all) economists take seriously the failings of using equilibrium theory for the purposes of policy.

Complexity scientists and complexity-aware economists loudly and publicly implored their colleagues to take seriously heterogeneous agents, social networks, feedbacks between agents and system-level variables, and evolutionary symmetry-breaking, both to better theorize and to better inform policy (Haldane 2009; Haldane and May 2011; Arthur 2014; Room 2011; Helbing and Kirman 2013; Colander et al 2014). Methodological purists requested a complete break from equilibrium theorizing for the purposes of conducting policy, and methodological pluralists said the new macroeconomics could accommodate the old "top-down" theories while including new "bottom-up" methods better able to account for growth processes and spontaneous orders (Colander and Kupers 2016). In the last few decades the tools of complexity science have been applied to the problem of public goods provision (Janssen and Ostrom 2006; Allouch 2015), understanding how policy might correct behavioral biases (Lombardi et al. 2012), and raising the efficiency of policy implementation (Pedell and Sterling 2011).

How to conduct policy in a complex system depends on which complexity economist you ask. One complexity vision, the architect vision, is characterized by specific surgical kinds of regulation, nudging, and bottom-up innovation priming or what Colander and Kupers (2016) call "getting the meta-conditions right" (see for overviews Arthur 2014; Colander and Kupers 2016; Room 2011, 2016; and Sunstein 2018 on nudging). Experts use bottom-up tools like nudging and priming to move the social system from a less socially desirable state to a more socially desirable state, where states are typically modeled as basins of attraction rather than equilibria. This is the vision I focus on in this article. Another vision, the normative vision exposited (separately) by Alan Kirman and Graham Room, rejects the modeling relevance of basins of attraction and other forms of convergence to more-or-less steady social states, seeing the scope for policy as including normative prescriptions like social equity and cohesion (Room 2016). Note that Room's ideas encompass both the architect and normative vision. I say relatively little about the normative vision, as it abandons traditionally 'economic' goals of improving subjectively determined welfare.

Still another vision, the creative vision exposited by Roger Koppl and Stuart Kauffman, is skeptical of both top-down and bottom-up roles for policy-makers due to the nonergodic evolutionary dynamics of creative economic systems, which tend to thwart most attempts at directly designing social outcomes even using algorithmic methods (Devins et al. 2017; Felin et al. 2014; Koppl et al. 2015; Koppl 2018). The creative vision sees individual, social, and political entrepreneurs as existing and interacting with each other and the system they seek to alter, and does not provide a specific scope for policy in the sense of a designer and her design. The creative approach is the approach I take in analyzing complex social systems and how policies affect them.

In the next section, I go through the primary tools of complexity economics in order to orient policy-making in a complex social system, and to contextualize the architect and creative approaches.

Then, we shall encounter the dragons.

3 The Cutting Edge of Complexity Economics

3.1 Agent-Based Modeling: Simulating the Entire Economy

Agent-based modeling (ABM) is an object-oriented programming methodology that allows programmers to encode heterogeneous characteristics of economic agents who then interact with each other based on a set of rules over time. The distribution of characteristics, the topology of the interaction space (network, plane, donut, etc.), how agents are activated (when they can act), and the rules of interaction between agents have significant consequences for how system variables in the simulation evolve through time (see Wilensky and Rand (2015) for an introduction and Gallegati and Kirman (2012) for a comparison between ABMs and traditional methods). Rather than starting with equations of interaction and a theoretical framework, like utility maximization in rational choice theory, then solving for the requisite equilibria, agents are programmed with characteristics and behaviors and a topology of connections, then the program is run for a certain (finite and typically large) number of steps. System variables are statistically determined at cross-sections of the evolution, to analyze the broader characteristics of the evolving system and to compare between runs of the system under different conditions.

ABMs have been proposed as ways to model an economy as a complex adaptive system under the acronym ACE, which stands for agent-based computational economics (Tesfatsion 2003). ABMs have the benefit of allowing for heterogeneity of agent characteristics, behaviors, and interactions. ABMs provide a mechanism for how myopic and only partially rational microeconomic interactions may result in macropatterned coordination over time without using linear aggregation. ABMs are mainly limited by their deterministic nature, which doesn't allow for much in the way of endogenous creativity and open-ended evolutionary behavior (see Devereaux and Wagner (2020) for a description of open-ended evolutionary economics).

One of the canonical examples of the kind of macropatterns explainable by ABMs is the Schelling segregation model, wherein agents who are not explicitly coordinating with each other to cluster in ethnicity-based groups and who do not have strong ethnicity-proximity preferences nevertheless end up tightly clustered in ethnicity-based groups (Schelling 1971). ABMs can be much more sophisticated than the Schelling segregation model, however, both in terms of the variety and topology of agent interactions, how the space of possible interactions changes through time, and in how agents understand or model the way their actions correlate with the outcomes they desire. Agent-based models were used to test the unique new solutions arrived at in evolutionary game theory (Axelrod 1997). Agent-based models describing the emergence of firms have large numbers of individual agents, and complicated dynamics with unstable equilibria (Axtell 1999).

3.2 Graph Theory: Interactions on a Network Topology

Like for ABMs, social networks give us a way of modeling heterogeneously interacting agents (in "integral" field space versus "nonintegral" discrete space, as described in Potts 2000). Graph theory is the mathematics behind analyzing social networks. Graph theory describes the properties of agents in a social network and the connections between agents. When agents act, we analyze the results of action in relation to the topology of the resulting graph, even if properties like agent attributes change while the graph itself remains constant. We can describe graphs through their shape via visual inspection, or through summary statistics when the graphs get large enough. Summary statistics include the diameter of the graph (the longest path-length between any given two nodes in the graph), the degree distribution (where high degree nodes have more connections than low-degree nodes), and average path-length (Jackson 2010). We can also look at the density and placement of microstructures, where microstructures are defined as minimal subgraphs like stars and directed triangles.

The use of graph theory and the abandonment of the representative agent was present in several "calls to arms" in reforming economic theory post-crisis (Haldane and May 2011; Helbing and Kirman 2013; Acemoglu et al. 2015). Others are more specific, suggesting that we model economic systems as locally-constructive sequential games (Tesfatsion 2017). Graph theory can naturally model information asymmetries, echo chamber effects, influence, information spread, and strategic learning by constructing interaction topologies where agents possess direct knowledge of their topological "neighbors" but not the entire set of all choosing agents (Jackson 2010).

Regardless of its theoretical standing in the economic community, networks are finding their use in many areas of economic analysis, including: financial networks (Eisenberg & Noe 2001), employment and inequality (Calvó-Armengol and Jackson 2004), education (Calvó-Armengol et al. 2009), firm collaboration (Schilling and Phelps 2007), "fake news" spread (Acemoglu et al. 2010), norm spread (Nakamaru and Levin 2004), and work team formation (Devereaux and Yuan 2019).

3.3 *Big Data and Machine Learning*

Our experiences are becoming more intensely colored by artificial intelligence trained on Big Data. Fitness apps remind us to record our weight and vibrate our wrists when we are too sedentary. Crime apps alert us to real-time crimes happening near our location. From anywhere in the world we can track the location and online activity of our kids (Wagenseil 2020), monitor and manage our "smart" home (Delaney and Colon 2020), and access footage from a dash cam. We are warned during our commute of debris on the road or speed traps ahead by apps like Waze. We can even report anti-social activity like the illegal sale or use of fireworks with a quick snap of a picture (Business Wire 2017). Algorithms match us with prospective partners (Harrington 2015).

Big Data is the term used for massive stores of data, often personalized, and the statistical and machine learning tools used to analyze that data. Which sites you visit, where you drive, your fitness records and sleep habits—all form a chunk of the data set that represents "you." Understanding this data in order to make plausible statements about how the data in your health records correlates with your fitness data, for instance, is another matter. Simple statistics and econometrics can be used if there's a particular model in mind, but often data analysis on massive data sets is handled using machine learning.

There are several different kinds of machine learning. One kind is deep learning, which applies successive and different representations to the data constituting the algorithm's "layers." How deep a model can be depends on how many layers (representations) it employs. The representations are learned from exposure to training data, and can number in the tens to hundreds (Chollet 2017: Chapter 1). Deep learning almost always utilizes a method of learning on training sets called artificial neural networks (ANNs).

It is likely that our lives will become even more enmeshed with advancements made in artificial intelligence as the potential and demand for AI as a helpful assistant, friend, personal trainer, and academic mentor is only beginning to be realized. The extent to which AI augments or replaces our behavior lies on a spectrum with voice-activated internet searches on one end—where AI augments our lives only at direct request—to automated cars on the other, where AI fully replaces us. In between, AI can be used to augment human behavior in ways beneficial in an individual's own judgment, beneficial to another individual, and beneficial in some measure of "social welfare." Sometimes these categories overlap, but not always. The use of AI, especially its privileged use, has the potential to benefit some groups and individuals at the expense of others.

AI has its roots in the 1950s, with luminaries such as cyberneticist Norbert Wiener and Ross Ashby essentially defining the early contours of the field. Economists quickly latched onto the promise of AI to provide the missing qualities as-yet-unprovidable by human programmers and mathematicians. In Alvin Hansen's 1951 text Business Cycles and National Income, Richard Goodwin expressed business cycle metaphors and elsewhere, Walrasian market dynamics, in term of servo-mechanism and feedback control (see Velupillai 2008, footnote 4, p 394; Hansen 1951: 436–8). Norbert Wiener (1948) text Cybernetics is listed as a common source of inspiration for Goodwin, Hansen, and Herbert Simon. The economist Jacob Marschak required Ross Ashby's (1956) cybernetics text in a course on economic information theory at Yale (Mirowski and Nik-Khah 2017). Cybernetics may provide such hope because its power lies outside the ability of human social engineers, which couldn't help but be convinced of their limitations amidst the failure of social engineering during Soviet bloc experimentation.

Why did the cybernetics fervor fizzle out in the first place? Cybernetics followed the rubric of symbolic AI, where humans enter rules (programs) of how to process data, and the output produces instructions or answers, for instance, how variables are causally related. Econometrics as normally practiced is symbolic AI, which presupposes a simple public governance mechanism whereby as long as you have the solution (variable causality) you can change it via the governance mechanism.

Economists who believe economies and policy ecosystems are complex, however, cannot rely on econometrics to direct policy action, as they do not presuppose that policies have simple implementations. Machine learning presupposes causality in the data (what the data means), and attempts to infer the rules that produce that presupposed known meaning. Symbolic AI presupposes knowledge of microrelationships. Machine learning presupposes knowledge of macrorelationships.

A designer is, in many ways, enabled and constrained by the nature of her tools. In the next section, we consider the plausible outcomes on positive and negative social institutions of utilizing these tools for social design. We shall then ask whether designers can effectively nudge societies towards higher "peaks" of social welfare (as suggested in Sunstein 2018; Colander and Kupers 2016; Room 2011, 2016), or whether they can impose normative values that protect and promote some other measure of overall social benefit (as suggested in Kirman 2016 and in Room 2011, 2016).

4 Here Be Dragons

Taking complexity in economic systems seriously means being serious about the suitability of analytical and computational tools used to analyze and form predictions on complex systems. In 2000, Jason Potts wrote the book Evolutionary Microeconomics, his attempt to build a foundation for a networks-based microeconomics. In his 2011 book Complexity and Economic Policy, Graham Room attempts to extend Potts's analysis to the policy level, though Room does not confine his analysis to interactions alone. Policies do not enter a vacuum, they enter a space inhabited by other policies and their effects. Models used by policy-makers must take into account the recursive nature of within-system policy applications that interact with themselves, other policies, preference formation, and the behaviors of agents (Room 2011). Richard Wagner's (2016) conception of entangled political economy includes recursion of the aforementioned affects, and also between agents and the institutions that themselves serve as the "rules of the game."

Room calls his architect-oriented vision of policy-making in a complex system "agile policy-making." Room conceives of his agile policy-maker as a "tuner," "energizer," and "steward" (ibid: 237–46). Tuners tinker with the shape and nature of the relationships between agents in the financial network as suggested in Haldane and May (2011), though some of the components of interest in their decompositions of complex phenomena may be themselves complex, like institutions. Energizers seek to create fertile environments for the creation and dissemination of knowledge and innovation. Elinor Ostrom gives an energizer-esque argument in favor of polycentric governance (2010). Stewards engage in "husbandry of the social fabric" (Room 2011: 241) to create and mold civilization based on shared normative values. For Colander and Kupers, an important role for policy-making in a complex system would be to "encourage people to adopt positive social norms" (Colander and Kupers 2016: 8). In Room's view, "[c]ivility must be built, it does not organise itself" (Room 2011: 241). Farmer and Geanakoplos (2009) concur, noting that since social laws are not natural in the sense of physical laws, "[e]conomics thus has a normative as well as a descriptive purpose" (17). Nudge theorists might be thought of as energizers to some extent, as detailed in Colander and Kupers (2016) in particular, and stewards in the sense of the libertarian paternalism of Thaler and Sunstein (2009).

Room's categories are explicitly anti-invisible hand, pro-design, and pro-paternalism; the new "complexity" paternalism, as it were. This is despite the evidence against design of legal systems (Devins et al. 2015), public policy based on traditional economic models (Velupillai 2007; Koppl et al. 2015), top-down design of economic systems (Mises 2020 [1920]; Hayek 1945), expert design in many applied and theoretical areas (Koppl 2018) and paternalism (Rizzo and Whitman 2009).

What, then, makes policy design using the tools and framework of complexity economics more effective? Is the use of these tools more effective? I argue that the tools of complexity economics are not, by themselves, unsinkable ships of effective paternalism. There are a great many "dragons" in those waters, or icebergs, if one wishes to continue the theme.

To be sure, most complexity economists are conservative about the scope for control and design of a complex social system. Colander and Kupers (2016), who see the role of the policy-maker more like that of Room's energizer, warn their readers that policy-making in the "complexity frame" and modern macroeconomic-based theorizing about policy are different animals.

Complexity science provides a fundamentally different policy frame— which we'll call the complexity frame, one in which the role of government is quite different. In the complexity frame, policy is designed to play a supporting role in an evolving ecostructure—it is not designed to control the system. (Colander and Kupers 2016: 9).

The role of the expert is undeniably defined by her tools, in the complexity frame perhaps even more so than in the equilibrium frame. Tuners, energizers, and stewards are participants in a complex system on which they act. They manifest in the system as influential bridge nodes, loci of polycentric governance, and as Big Players (Granovetter 1977; Koppl 2002). Their participation shapes and warps the configuration of social and individual incentives, by design and by consequence.

Let's start our investigation of the dragons that lay in wait in the dangerous waters of public policy-making in a complex world. Our first dragon represents what Richard Wagner (2016) calls "entangled political economy." This dragon is a formidable foe even in the gentler waters of neoclassical analysis; in a complex social system, it threatens to overturn the unsinkable ship of agile policy-making.

4.1 The Cybernetic Dragon: Or, How Agile Policy-Making Is Entangled with Agile Self-Organization

I take a broad view of design in order to accommodate the vision of complexity economists who see themselves more like social entrepreneurs than social engineers, as exemplified by Room's (2011) concept of agile policy-making and Colander and Kupers' (2016: 8) concept of "laissez-faire activism." I do so, however, while formally acknowledging the process of agile self-organization as exemplified by F. A. Hayek's concept of catallaxy (1973) and Elinor Ostrom's concept of polycentricity (2010), and by placing designers inside their design (Wagner 2010). The task is to then inquire about the appropriate degree of design a system can bear without generating too many perverse incentives that catalyze self-interested behavior towards exploitation of group by group, and/or destroy the positive externalities of self-organization.

Agile self-organization is the use of tools like new technologies to better solve social and individual problems in decentralized, undesigned ways. Agile policy-making is the use of the tools of complexity science to design an ecostructure of sorts which then better enables individuals to be better off in their own lights.

A long time ago Koopmans said that it would not matter if people's preferences and choices changed at random so long as there were many of them and the individual changes were sufficiently independent...[Föllmer] showed...that equilibrium prices would not be modified even if individuals' preferences were affected by their neighbors' provided that the influence was not too strong. The policy problem is to determine what is "too strong" and when we are likely to be in such situations. Finding answers to these questions is important because once local interaction has a significant influence on the behavior of economic agents, all sorts of aggregate effects can appear. (Kirman 2006: xix).

Taking interactions into account in a responsible way requires putting the public actor inside the system he is attempting to intervene upon. Public actors and other high-degree central agents display great influence on which kinds of information and from where is allowed to travel through the network, as discussed in Burt's theory of structural holes and Granovetter's concept of influential bridge nodes between community clusters (Burt 2004; Granovetter 1977). Decentralized complex social systems are not chaotic; they are highly organized. Effective intervention conceivably improves the ability of system agents to coordinate and thus realize their ends. Agile policy-making uses complexity science and new technologies like algorithmic decision-guiding processes to design an ecostructure to enable individuals to be better off in their own lights. System agents, who have the same complexity tools available to experts in addition to epistemological advantages, also seek to alter the system to favor individual and social goals through agile self-organization.

Policies do not enter a vacuum; they enter a space inhabited by policy-makers and other policies, and an ecology of self-organized and evolutionary solutions to social problems. Intervening affects the ability of the system to self-organize for the benefit of the average participant, and the success or unintended consequences of existing policy measures. To what extent could a public fitness tracker bundled with the sale of every new phone crowd out the creation of other fitness trackers conceivably better suited to advance the ends of any given user? In especially in a sector burgeoning with creativity, publicly mandated apps or features could freeze progress at an evolutionarily suboptimal level.

Furthermore, agile policy-making, though potentially able to realize the goals of policymakers, may alter the nature and effectiveness of agile self-organization by changing system incentives and therefore foment the creation of rents, encourage coalition formation, reward conflict relative to cooperation, and encourage social entrepreneurs to develop public rather than polycentric solutions (Tullock 1967; Devereaux 2019). Especially in tech sectors that burgeon with creativity, publicly mandated apps and algorithmic solutions could freeze progress as a suboptimal level (Devereaux 2020).

Suitably constructed algorithms have the ability to deeply influence the behaviors of those subjected to them (Yeung 2017, 2018). Automatic decision systems exist at the public and private level, mostly as risk assessment tools: many mortgage applications rely on automated processes to determine whether a mortgage is granted or denied, as do parole decisions. Recently, the power and influence of these algorithms—specifically, their ability to discriminate against entire groups of people (Pasquale 2015)—has been a subject of a so-called algorithm responsibility bill proposed by New York City and supported by the New York division of the ACLU (Coldewey 2017).

Recall how machine learning allows one to infer the macrorelationships in a system, or the rules that generate the observed behaviors. Are theorists then free to use these rules of the game to tinker the system into different outcomes? Not quite—the problem being that there are several vectors in which bias can enter any machine learning task. The first is through data bias, as data can be incomplete, representative not of objective relationships but pre-existing human biases that are subject themselves to change; the next is through developer bias, where the developer trains a supervised set in an erroneous fashion or uses an insufficient method to correctly identify categorizations in an unsupervised setting, and the third is through epistemological bias, which represents the conundrum of inexorable systemic movement into the unknowable.

Which processes best ameliorate the negative effects of these biases—agile policy-making, or agile self-organization? Suppose a policymaker wishes to use algorithmic governance to nudge people from being too sedentary. It would be disadvantageous to the policymaker if the market was already saturated with private fitness apps without the kind of automatic (default, coercive) sedentary nudging he envisioned. He and his economic advisors might call this a "suboptimal social outcome." Private algorithms borne of agile-self organization therefore compete with, blockade, and substitute for public algorithms borne of agile policy-making.

On its face, adopting algorithmic governance to better target populations in apparent need of intervention sounds like an improvement to the undesigned marketplace of algorithmic solutions, which may or may not produce the apparent welfare-enhancing nudges on its own. But the burden of proof as to the welfare benefits of a publicly funded fitness app with anti-sedentary nudging relative to existing fitness applications lays with the policymaker. If consumers are already are seeking assistance to reach and maintain health goals, there's no particular behavioral economics argument for why public apps have an edge over private apps, as the welfare standard is whether people are made better off according to their own judgment—which they exercise when choosing one of the many fitness apps available versus another. That is, if they're not choosing an app with a default alarm to nudge them to stand up every 10 min, perhaps it's because they don't want one, not because they don't know what's best for them.

A good deal of the power and promise in AI is in its ability to enact vast changes on human systems in any number of imagined directions very quickly. As Karen Yeung points out in her 2017 article on cybernetic nudges she calls "hypernudges," algorithms that affect huge numbers of people (like all Facebook users) have a huge amount of power to affect individual behaviors. And while Yeung sounds the alarm for private and public hypernudges alike, the form and consequences of these two kinds of hypernudges are not symmetric in the framework of entangled political economy. The "hyper" in her definition of hypernudge comes from the well-connectedness of the nudger to her nudgees. As discussed in the example of the "tuner," the more well-connected an agent, the more influence the agent has over the behaviors of other agents in the network. Public actors can compel full connectivity to all agents in the system, while private agents do not have that power. Anyone can choose to use or not to use Facebook.

Public hypernudges, on the other hand, would propagate to you by first earning not your attention, but the attention of politically powerful special interests. The ability to compel connections attracts rent-seekers and exacerbates coalition formation (the same mechanism as explicated in Hebert and Wagner 2018). Any gains in agent welfare (according to their own judgment) experienced by better targeting intervention populations to improve their utility may very well be wiped out by massing special interests to use the same algorithmic targeting tools to extract benefits from this rapt audience.

4.2 *The Monstrous Neoclassical Hybrid*

One of the most dangerous 'dragons' is the least suspecting. He emerges from the creation of theoretically inconsistent policy measures, whose goals are developed in reference to a theoretical frame that is mathematically incompatible with the theoretical frame used to develop the process to attain those goals. I touched upon this dragon earlier when referencing nudge theory, but its fiery breath has left nearly no areas of theoretical economics unscorched.

Two main points constitute this dragon: (1) the noncomputability of neoclassical equilibria combined with the necessity for effective policy, particularly algorithmic policy, to be computable, and (2) the incompatibility between integral and nonintegral theoretical frames. Much of the first point about noncomputability I discussed in Sect. 2, but it bears reminding that a computable process is a series of steps generated by some programmable function or algorithm. One need not "compile" the set of instructions that runs the program process using an actual computer: it may be simply a series of steps executed by people (administrators, in the case of public policy) whose inputs (endogenous and exogenous) lead to the required outputs at each step so that the process can reliably continue to its ultimate predicted conclusion.

To take up the question of agile policy-making's effectiveness, we must define first what we mean by effective. When Vela K. Velupillai took up the same task in his 2007 review of policy on simple and complex systems, he demonstrated using a computability argument that if effective means welfare-enhancing in the neoclassical sense, then effective policy in a complex economy is impossible (Velupillai 2007). Koppl et al. (2015) demonstrate a similar result with respect to policy-making over time, noting that the phase space of economic choices is nonergodic due to the actions of creative entrepreneurs, who continually introduce novel choices into the system such that maximization over time is impossible for both individuals and societies.

Policy-makers can successfully use the tools of complexity science to influence social behavior in the direction they desire. Consider the literature on the success of some nudge-style interventions, like nudges to increase savings and retirement plan participation widely cited by nudge proponents (Madrian and Shea 2001; Thaler and Benartzi 2004; Carroll et al. 2009). Such early successes and the widespread popularity of Thaler and Sunstein's (2009) Nudge have led to the instantiation of governmental 'nudge units,' like the United Kingdom's Behavioral Insights Team, Ireland's Behavioral Economics Unit, and other nudge units in the United States, Canada, Australia, Germany, and the Netherlands.

But are nudges "effective" in the neoclassical sense of improving social welfare? This is not at all clear. The success of nudges is measured in whether they realize goals like increasing savings rates or tax compliance in certain demographics, not whether they improve the welfare of agents representing those demographics. Let's not make the mistake of conflating subjective welfare for objective goals.

Policies are often written in the following way: first, enact a soda tax of 50% so that (presumably) obese people will consume less and therefore (presumably) lose weight. The soda tax is related to weight loss through a process, which is determined by a belief in the relationship between a) weight and sugar intake, b) weight and health, c) health and social well-being, d) weight and income class, e) the elasticity of soda consumption in that income class. If any of these relationships aren't as strong or simple as conceived by the policy, the policy will not work. Indeed, relationships a) and b) are rather complicated even though they are commonly believed to be strong and simple. If obesity isn't the causal factor of the health issues the soda tax is meant to ameliorate—and it may be that hyperinsulinemia is the causal factor of both obesity and type 2 diabetes, as well as a host of other previously believed to be comorbities of obesity (Noakes 2018; Erion & Corkey 2017)—then targeting obesity as the metric of the success of the policy is the wrong strategy; rather, lowering barriers for people to purchase cheap insulin or to improve testing for the earliest stages of hyperinsulinemia would be more beneficial to the health outcomes of these very same populations. If we think of an algorithm like a nested recursive function with endogenous and exogenous inputs, we can model a three-step algorithmic process like:

$$f\left(g\left(h\left(x\right),y\right),z\right)=a \tag{1}$$

where $h(x)$ is the first endogenous input to function g; x, y, and z are exogenous inputs; and a is the intended outcome of the process.

Imagine that x represents an original population with a high level of risk for various indicators of ill health. Eventually, through several actions upon the initial population x, it evolves into a final population a that, if the process works, has the desired lower level of risk. If the model that relates the population to an intervention at any stage of the process is incorrect—say, g' instead of g—then the process will result in some $a' \neq a$:

$$f\left(g'\left(h\left(x\right),y\right),z\right)=a'$$

Therefore, in order to realize the intended outcomes of policies, policy-makers require a practical and approximately correct computable process with which to realize those intended outcomes. Very often, as we've seen in the case of soda taxes, the science itself isn't settled on the causal relationship between population characteristics (like obesity) and desired outcomes (like better population health). Correlations are fairly easy to produce in most areas of scientific inquiry, but effective policies require knowing not just correlations but causality.

Empirical relationships are only one part of how economists who advise policy-makers devise their recommendations. Economists also rely on analytical models, and all economists are trained first and foremost in neoclassical modeling using the basic mathematical infrastructure laid by Arrow-Debreu, and on game theory with solutions in the core. Often, policy advice comes in the following fashion: construct a population of agents that are rational in the neoclassical sense of having the computational and cognitive ability to compute fixed points in an economy-wide fashion, but with certain constraints the modelers believe better represents realistic choice in a certain domain of interest (like employees choosing effort levels in informationally asymmetric employment situations). Then, compare the resultant level of aggregated individually optimized utilities (choices of effort levels made by each individual) to the planner's problem of setting a universal effort level to optimize aggregate utility. If the planner can do better than individuals choosing on their own, we have a strong case for third party intervention. Even better, we have a policy: change effort levels (or whatever the variables of interest are) in the treatment population to more closely match the theoretically optimal effort level.

And here is where our ship founders. Why? Consider Eq. 1. The analytical model presumes to reasonably approximate the target population x with "suboptimal" effort levels in its model setup. People are reasonably described as rational choosers, and the variable of interest can be reasonably isolated from other factors and relationships. We then analytically derive a desired outcome, a population a with "optimal" effort level.

Notice what is missing? Only the entire process that transforms x into a…!

Furthermore, it could be that there is no practical, plausibly executable process to transform x into a, because we never proved one exists. We only proved that $W(a) > W(x)$, where W is the social welfare function. Proof of existence using the Law of the Excluded Middle produces a process with the form of Eq. 2:

$$h_n\left(\ldots\left(h_3\left(h_2\left(h_1\left(x\right),y_1\right),y_2\right),y_3\right)\ldots,y_n\right)=a \quad (2)$$

where the h_i, are unknown transformations of endogenous inputs and unknown exogenous vectors of inputs y_i, and n is an unknown level of steps. The only knowns are the original population x and its features, and the desired population a and its features. And even if we are able to find a computational process to transform x into a such that $W(a) > W(x)$, the simplest salient form of this process may still be too computationally hard to execute.

The second feature of a monstrous neoclassical hybrid is the incompatibility between informationally integral theoretical frames, in which neoclassical welfare targets are deduced, and informationally nonintegral theoretical frames, that is, the social and political networks in which policies actually operate.

It is not enough to place agents in a network, generate system-level statistics given simple maximizing behavior, observe a relationship between topological features and one of the system-level statistics and then generate a policy conclusion based on those observations. Interventions into self-organized, nonintegral systems need to understand the trade-offs between, say, topological characteristics of the system that correlate negatively to a given statistic, and how changing those characteristics alters to proper function and self-organizational nature of the system itself.

I take the example of such an analysis from Acemoglu et al. 2015, where the authors model the relationship between how quickly a "contagion" – like bank failures – can spread in an interbank network, and the topology of the network. Their model is based on the framework developed by Eisenberg and Noe (2001). Define the resiliency $R(G)$ of a network G as the minimality of the extent of the spread of the contagion or, in our example, the cascade of bank failures. Formally:

$$R(G) = 1 - 1/(n-1)E[\text{extent of a cascade}]$$

where E is the expectation, the extent of a cascade refers to the ultimate number of new cases created by a single failed node (the initial node does not count), and where n = the number of nodes.

Under this definition, the most cascade-resilient network is $R(G) = 1$. But this G is the network with no edges, and hence this network cannot carry any information between the nodes.

As noted in Gutfraind (2012: 41), "[T]he objective of designing cascade resilience conflicts with other features of the network." Cascades resilience trades off with the informational efficiency of a network and with how the network develops dynamically to minimize transaction costs between the nodes. Glasserman and Young (2015) note in particular that a weakness of models built using the Eisenberg-Noe framework is their inability to account for how links form, that is, "the dynamic process by which financial institutions enter into obligations to one another in the first place." (ibid: 384).

Consider instead another metric of a network, called fitness. Fitness characterizes a system or state of being based on its ability to realize the goals of the agents in the system and its stability. Gutfraind (2012) defines the overall fitness $F(G)$ of a network G as

$$F(G) = rR(G) + (1-r)W(G) \tag{3}$$

where r is a weight in [0, 1], the informational efficiency of the network is $W(G)$, and the resilience of the network is $R(G)$. Equation 3 describes the tradeoff between resilience and efficiency such that tuning r results in some maximum fitness $F(G)$—though, as cascade risk isn't constant, tuning would have to occur at regular intervals and when financial conditions are changing. Even networks with many distinct clusters naturally protective against system-wide contagion (high modularity) can experience system-wide contagion when cascade risk crosses a certain threshold (the percolation transition).

Cascades are common in networks with the degree of complexity seen in social and interbank networks (Gutfraind 2012). Cascades are associated with negative phenomena, like bank failures, and with positive phenomena, like the sharing of funny, pleasant, or important messages— memes—through social media. A network's ability to host cascades signifies a high level of informational efficiency. The mere possibility of cascades is not reason alone to change a network's topology, as nearly all networks created by people—friend networks, employment and academic networks, institutional networks, banking networks, business networks—are complex enough to host cascades.

5 Conclusion: What Should Complexity Economists Do?

In The Constitution of Liberty, F. A. Hayek promotes the seedlike version of what bottom-up complexity theorists now call nudge (in the more generalized, less behavioral sense of the word). He likens the lawmaker's duty–a lawmaker who sits entirely outside of the system he acts upon–to create the conditions in which people, when acting in their own self-interest, act in the best interest of the entire system. Hayek employs the metaphor of a crystalline phase transition, suggesting that the task of the policy-maker is to design the conditions from which good economic outcomes can then emerge (Hayek 1960: 230–1). Hayek seems to believe that policy-makers can enable a "crystal" to form, though they are generally no good at commanding the crystal into being. To a great extent, Hayek is answering the question of what economists should do when they understand the economy from a complexity perspective where epistemological considerations are paramount (Hayek 1937, 1945, 1960, 1964, 1967).

A fair characterization of the complexity-economist-turned-agile-policy-maker is not too far off Hayek's mark. Today's agile policy-maker seeks to implement algorithmic nudge in an entangled political economy characterized by Big Players, coalitions and competing modes of governance, in the hope of generating a phase transition from a lower to a higher level of social welfare. Is this phase transition achieved?

There is nothing special about the epistemological conditions faced by the agile policy-maker; they may have Big Data, but still lack the knowledge that "by its very nature, cannot enter into statistics" (Hayek 1945); they may have social network theory, but still cannot apprehend all the ways in which evolutionary and social knowledge presents itself (Hayek 1960; Koppl 2018); they have algorithms whose ends are programmed into their assumptions and thus their assumptions reflect their ends, the ends of the designer.

Agile policy-making may very likely enhance coalitional power and destabilize an ecology characterized by competing modes of governance. In terms of polycentricity, agile policy-making has the potential to displace the locus of governance, thereby concentrating decision-making power in fewer hands and effectively subverting the gains historically enjoyed by a thriving ecology of public and private governance.

This brings me to my final observation: why shouldn't Hayekian rules that enable us to make ourselves better off in our own judgments emanate from the evolving and adaptive discovery procedure characterized by the creative vision of policy in a complex economic system? Hayek believes that plans are better made through such a creative process; why not rules? Perhaps complexity economists who advise policy-makers should think more deeply on this point, lest we forever be chained to the dragons of design.

References

Acemoglu, D., Ozdaglar, A., & Parandeh Gheibi, A. (2010). Spread of (mis)information in social networks. *Games and Economic Behavior, 70*(2), 194–227.

Acemoglu, D., Ozdaglar, A., & Tahbaz-Salehi, A. (2015). Systemic risk and stability in financial networks. *American Economic Review, 105*(2), 564–608.

Allouch, N. (2015). On the private provision of public goods on networks. *Journal of Economic Theory, 157*, 527–552.

Arthur, W. B. (2014). *Complexity and the economy*. Oxford: Oxford University Press.

Ashby, W. R. (1956). *An introduction to cybernetics*. Hoboken: Wiley.

Axelrod, R. (1997). *The complexity of cooperation: Agent-based models of competition and collaboration*. Princeton: Princeton University Press.

Axtell, R. (1999). *The emergence of firms in a population of agents: Local increasing returns, unstable Nash equilibria, and power law size distributions*. Santa Fe: Santa Fe Institute.

Babichenko, Y., & Rubinstein, A. (2016). Communication complexity of approximate Nash equilibria. *arXiv*. preprint arXiv:1608.06580.

Burt, R. S. (2004). Structural holes and good ideas. *American Journal of Sociology, 110*(2), 349–399.

Business Wire (June 13, 2017). Use Illegal Fireworks? Smile! You've Been "Nailed"! Business Wire. Available at: https://www.businesswire.com/news/home/20170613005523/en/Illegal-Fireworks-Smile%21-You%E2%80%99ve-%E2%80%9CNailed%E2%80%9D%21. Accessed 1 Sep 2020.

Calvó-Armengol, A., & Jackson, M. O. (2004). The effects of social networks on employment and inequality. *American Economic Review, 94*(3), 426–454.

Calvó-Armengol, A., Patacchini, E., & Zenou, Y. (2009). Peer effects and social networks in education. *The Review of Economic Studies, 76*(4), 1239–1267.

Carroll, G. D., Choi, J. J., Laibson, D., Madrian, B. C., & Metrick, A. (2009). Optimal defaults and active decisions. *The Quarterly Journal of Economics, 124*(4), 1639–1674.

Chollet, F. (2017). *Deep learning with python*. Shelter Island: Manning Publications.

Colander, D., & Kupers, R. (2016). *Complexity and the art of public policy: Solving society's problems from the bottom up*. Princeton: Princeton University Press.

Colander, D., Follmer, H., Haas, A., Goldberg, M., Juselius, K., Kirman, A., & Sloth, B. (2014). The financial crisis and the systemic failure of academic economics. The economics of economists: Institutional setting, individual incentives, and future. *Prospects, 21*(2–3), 344.

Coldewey, D. (December 12, 2017). New York City moves to establish algorithm-monitoring task force. Tech Crunch. Available at: https://techcrunch.com/2017/12/12/new-york-city-moves-to--establish-algorithm-monitoring-task-force/. Accessed 1 Sep 2020.

Devereaux, A., & Yuan, X. (2019). Visualizing the division of knowledge: A simulation of the formation of transactive memory systems. Available at SSRN 3326779.

Devereaux, A. N. (2019). Approaching the singularity behind the veil of incomputability: On algorithmic governance, the economist-as-expert, and the piecemeal circumnavigation of the administrative state. *Cosmos & Taxis, 7*(1+2).

Devereaux, A. N. (2020). *The digital wild west: On social entrepreneurship in extended reality*. SSRN working paper. https://papers.ssrn.com/sol3/papers.cfm?abstract_id=3352956. Accessed 18 Feb 2020.

Devereaux, A. N., & Wagner, R. E. (2020). Contrasting visions for macroeconomic theory: DSGE and OEE. *The American Economist, 65*(1), 28–50.

Devins, C., Koppl, R., Kauffman, S., & Felin, T. (2015). Against design. *Arizona Law Review, 47*, 609.

Devins, C., Felin, T., Kauffman, S., & Koppl, R. (2017). The law and big data. *Cornell JL & Public Policy, 27*, 357.

Delaney, J. R., Colon, A. (April 9, 2020). The Best Smart Home Security Systems for 2020. PC Magazine. Available at: https://www.pcmag.com/picks/the-best-smart-home-security-systems. Accessed 1 Sep 2020.

Eisenberg, L., & Noe, T. H. (2001). Systemic risk in financial systems. *Management Science, 47*(2), 236–249.

Erion, K. A., & Corkey, B. E. (2017). Hyperinsulinemia: A cause of obesity? *Current Obesity Reports, 6*(2), 178–186.

Farmer, J. D., & Foley, D. (2009). The economy needs agent-based modelling. *Nature, 460*(7256), 685.

Farmer, J. D., & Geanakoplos, J. (2009). The virtues and vices of equilibrium and the future of financial economics. *Complexity, 14*(3), 11–38.

Felin, T., Kauffman, S., Koppl, R., & Longo, G. (2014). Economic opportunity and evolution: Beyond landscapes and bounded rationality. *Strategic Entrepreneurship Journal, 8*(4), 269–282.

Gallegati, M., & Kirman, A. (2012). Reconstructing economics: Agent based models and complexity. *Complexity Economics, 1*(1), 5–31.

Glasserman, P., & Young, H. P. (2015). How likely is contagion in financial networks? *Journal of Banking & Finance, 50*, 383–399.

Goodwin, R. M. (1951). Econometrics in business cycle analysis. In *Alvin Hansen (1951, 1964 – Expanded edition): Business cycles and national income* (pp. 417–468). New York: WW Norton & Company.

Granovetter, M. S. (1977). The strength of weak ties. In S. Leinhardt (Ed.), *Social networks* (pp. 347–367).

Gutfraind, A. (2012). Optimizing network topology for cascade resilience. In *Handbook of optimization in complex networks* (pp. 37–59). New York: Springer.

Haldane, A. G. (2009). *Rethinking the financial network*. Speech delivered at the financial student association, Amsterdam, April 28.

Haldane, A. G., & May, R. M. (2011). Systemic risk in banking ecosystems. *Nature, 469*, 351–355.

Hansen, A. H. (1951). *Business cycles and national income*. New York: WW Norton & Company.

Harrington, R. (Feb 13 2015). Dating services tinker with the algorithms of love. *Scientific American*. Available at: https://www.scientificamerican.com/article/dating-services-tinker-with-the-algorithms-of-love/. Accessed 24 Feb 2018.
Hayek, F. A. (1937). Economics and knowledge. *Economica, 4*(13), 33–54.
Hayek, F. A. (1945). The use of knowledge in society. *The American Economic Review, 35*(4), 519–530.
Hayek, F. (1960). The Constitution of Liberty. Chicago: University of Chicago Press.
Hayek, F. A. (1964). The theory of complex phenomena. In *The critical approach to science and philosophy* (pp. 332–349).
Hayek, F. A. (1967). *Studies in philosophy, politics and economics* (p. 100). London: Routledge & Kegan Paul.
Hayek, F. A. (1973). *Law, legislation and liberty, volume 1: Rules and order*. Chicago: University of Chicago Press.
Hebert, D. J., & Wagner, R. E. (2018). Political parties: Insights from a tri-planar model of political economy. *Constitutional Political Economy, 29*(3), 253–267.
Helbing, D., & Kirman, A. (2013). Rethinking economics using complexity theory. *Real-world Economics Review, 64*.
Jackson, M. O. (2010). *Social and economic networks*. Princeton: Princeton University Press.
Janssen, M. A., & Ostrom, E. (2006). Empirically based, agent-based models. *Ecology and Society, 11*(2).
Kirman, A. (2004). Economics and complexity. *Advances in Complex Systems, 7*, 139–155.
Kirman, A. (2006). Foreword. In D. Colander (Ed.), *Post walrasian macroeconomics*. Cambridge: Cambridge University Press.
Koppl, R. (2002). *Big players and the economic theory of expectations*. Springer.
Koppl, R. (2018). *Expert failure*. Cambridge: Cambridge University Press.
Koppl, R., Kauffman, S., Felin, T., & Longo, G. (2015). Economics for a creative world. *Journal of Institutional Economics, 11*(1), 1–31.
Lachmann, L. M. (1976). From Mises to Shackle: An essay on Austrian economics and the kaleidic society. *Journal of Economic Literature, 14*(1), 54–62.
Lewis, A. A. (1985). On effectively computable realizations of choice functions: Dedicated to professors Kenneth J. arrow and Anil Nerode. *Mathematical Social Sciences, 10*(1), 43–80.
Lombardi, L., Paich, M., & Rao, A. (2012). *Behavioral simulations: Using agent-based modeling to understand policyholder behaviors.*. Society of Actuaries.
Madrian, B. C., & Shea, D. F. (2001). The power of suggestion: Inertia in 401(k) participation and savings behavior. *The Quarterly Journal of Economics, 116*(4), 1149–1187.
Mirowski, P., & Nik-Khah, E. (2017). *The knowledge we have lost in information: The history of information in modern economics*. Oxford University Press.
Mises, L. V. (2020 [1920]). Economic Calculation in the Socialist Commonwealth. Auburn, AL: Ludwig von Mises Institute.
Nakamaru, M., & Levin, S. A. (2004). Spread of two linked social norms on complex interaction networks. *Journal of Theoretical Biology, 230*(1), 57–64.
Noakes, T. D. (2018). So what comes first: The obesity or the insulin resistance? And which is more important? *Clinical Chemistry, 64*(1), 7–9.
Novak, M. (2018). Entangled political economy: A general introduction. In *Inequality* (pp. 29–54). Cham: Palgrave Macmillan.
Ostrom, E. (2010). Beyond markets and states: Polycentric governance of complex economic systems. *American Economic Review, 100*(3), 641–672.
Papadimitriou, C. H. (1994). On the complexity of the parity argument and other inefficient proofs of existence. *Journal of Computer and System Sciences, 48*(3), 498–532.
Pasquale, F. (2015). *The black box society*. Cambridge: Harvard University Press.
Pedell, S., & Sterling, L. (2011). The benefits of agent-based motivation models in policy formulation and implementation. In *International conference on autonomous agents and multiagent systems* (pp. 113–127). Berlin/Heidelberg: Springer.

Potts, J. (2000). *Evolutionary microeconomics*. Edward Elgar Publishing.

Rizvi, S. A. T. (2006). The Sonnenschein-mantel-Debreu results after thirty years. *History of Political Economy, 38*(Suppl_1), 228–245.

Rizzo, M. J., & Whitman, D. G. (2009). Little brother is watching you: New paternalism on the slippery slopes. *Arizona Law Review, 51*, 685.

Romer, P. (2016). The trouble with macroeconomics. *The American Economist, 20*, 1–20.

Room, G. (2011). *Complexity, institutions and public policy: Agile decision-making in a turbulent world*. Edward Elgar Publishing.

Room, G. (2016). *Agile actors on complex terrains: Transformative realism and public policy*. Routledge.

Schelling, T. C. (1971). Dynamic models of segregation. *Journal of Mathematical Sociology, 1*(2), 143–186.

Schelling, T. (1978). *Micromotives and macrobehavior*. New York: WW Norton & Company.

Schilling, M. A., & Phelps, C. C. (2007). Interfirm collaboration networks: The impact of large-scale network structure on firm innovation. *Management Science, 53*(7), 1113–1126.

Shackle, G. L. (1972). Economics and Epistemics. New Brunswick, NJ: Transaction Publishers.

Shafer, W., & Sonnenschein, H. (1982). Market demand and excess demand functions. *Handbook of Mathematical Economics, 2*, 671–693.

Simon, H. A. (1972). Theories of bounded rationality. *Decision and Organization, 1*(1), 161–176.

Smith, V. L. (2003). Constructivist and ecological rationality in economics. *American Economic Review, 93*(3), 465–508.

Smith, A. (2010(1752)). *The theory of moral sentiments*. Penguin.

Stiglitz, J. E. (2018). Where modern macroeconomics went wrong. *Oxford Review of Economic Policy, 34*(1–2), 70–106.

Sunstein, C. R. (2018). Better off, as judged by themselves: a comment on evaluating nudges. *International Review of Economics, 65*(1), 1–8.

Tesfatsion, L. (2003). Agent-based computational economics: Modeling economies as complex adaptive systems. *Information Sciences, 149*(4), 262–268.

Tesfatsion, L. (2017). Modeling economic systems as locally-constructive sequential games. *Journal of Economic Methodology, 24*(4), 384–409.

Thaler, R. H., & Benartzi, S. (2004). Save more tomorrowTM: Using behavioral economics to increase employee saving. *Journal of Political Economy, 112*(S1), 164–187.

Thaler, R. H., & Sunstein, C. R. (2009). *Nudge: Improving decisions about health, wealth, and happiness*. Penguin.

Tullock, G. (1967). The welfare costs of tariffs, monopolies, and theft. *Economic Inquiry, 5*(3), 224–232.

Veblen, T. (1898). Why is economics not an evolutionary science?. *The Quarterly Journal of Economics, 12*(4), 373–397.

Velupillai, K. V. (2007). The impossibility of an effective theory of policy in a complex economy. In *Complexity hints for economic policy* (pp. 273–290). Milano: Springer.

Velupillai, K. V. (2008). *Computable foundations for economics* (p. 394). Taylor and Francis.

Velupillai, K. V. (2016). Seven kinds of computable and constructive infelicities in economics. *New Mathematics and Natural Computation, 12*(03), 219–239.

Wagner, R. E. (2010). *Mind, society, and human action: Time and knowledge in a theory of social-economy*. Routledge.

Wagner, R. E. (2016). *Politics as a peculiar business: Insights from a theory of entangled political economy*. Edward Elgar Publishing.

Wagenseil, P. (August 24, 2020). The best parental control apps for Android and iPhone 2020. Tom's Guide. Available at: https://www.tomsguide.com/us/best-parental-control-apps,review-2258.html. Accessed 1 Sep 2020.

Wicksell, K. (1898, [1936]), Interest and Prices, translated by Richard F. Kahn, Macmillan, London.

Wiener, N. (1948). *Cybernetics, or control and communication in the animal and the machine*. New York: Wiley.

Wilensky, U., & Rand, W. (2015). *An introduction to agent-based modeling: Modeling natural, social, and engineered complex systems with NetLogo*. MIT Press.
Yeung, K. (2017). 'Hypernudge': Big data as a mode of regulation by design. *Information, Communication & Society, 20*(1), 118–136.
Yeung, K. (2018). Algorithmic regulation: A critical interrogation. *Regulation & Governance, 12*(4), 505–523.

Taxonomy of Entrepreneurship – A Means-Oriented Approach

Marta Podemska-Mikluch

Abstract The growth of entrepreneurship literature spurred a discussion on the distinct characteristics of the different types of entrepreneurship, with most attention being given to market, social, and political entrepreneurship. In organizing the inquiry around these supposedly distinct types of entrepreneurship, scholars tend to focus on the goals entrepreneurs pursue: market entrepreneurs are portrayed as driven by profit, political entrepreneurs are driven by rents, and social entrepreneurs are thought to be driven by other, supposedly less venal, motivations. This paper presents the shortcomings of this ends-oriented taxonomy and offers an alternative approach for organizing inquiry, one that originates from Richard Wagner's framework of Entangled Political Economy and his distinction between voluntary and involuntary investors. I argue that instead of focusing on the ends, the taxonomy of entrepreneurship should focus on the means, in particular, on whether the resources that support the venture were obtained through cooperation or coercion.

Keywords Taxonomy of entrepreneurship · Categories of entrepreneurship Social entrepreneurship · Political entrepreneurship · Conventional entrepreneurship · Means-oriented · Ends-oriented

1 Introduction

Taxonomy is usually defined as the practice and science of classification of things or concepts, including the principles that underlie such classification. The purpose of a taxonomy is to make complex subjects more approachable, to increase shared understanding, and by doing so, to facilitate further inquiry. So, taxonomies are only as useful as their ability to advance understanding and accelerate learning. But when taxonomies emerge before the subject is well understood, they will not advance understanding but instead might hamper it. Currently, the entrepreneurship literature distinguishes between different types of entrepreneurship primarily based

M. Podemska-Mikluch (✉)
Gustavus Adolphus College, St. Peter, MN, USA
e-mail: mpodemsk@gustavus.edu

D. J. Hebert, D. W. Thomas (eds.), *Emergence, Entanglement, and Political Economy*, Studies in Public Choice 38, https://doi.org/10.1007/978-3-030-56088-1_5

on the goals pursued by entrepreneurs. Such is the case with the distinction between market entrepreneurship, social entrepreneurship, and political entrepreneurship. Market entrepreneurs are thought to pursue profits, political entrepreneurs to seek rents, and social entrepreneurs are thought to be driven by the desire to eradicate social ills (Dacin et al. 2010; Klein et al. 2010). Numerous other adjectives have been added to describe different forms of entrepreneurship, leading researchers to investigate ideological, institutional, and cultural entrepreneurship. In making these distinctions scholars focus primarily on the goals entrepreneurs pursue and, to a lesser extent, on the socio-institutional environments in which they operate.

As I argue in this paper, the distinct ends-based categories of market, political, and social entrepreneurship are closely related to the additive political economy approach. As described by Wagner, the additive political economy treats polity and economy as independent spheres of activity (Wagner 2016). In the framework of additive political economy, the role of government is to improve on the imperfect outcomes generated by the market, to intervene where the market fails. Conceptualizations of social and political entrepreneurship are born out of this additive understanding of the relationship between markets and the government. Political entrepreneurship is thought to emerge as entrepreneurs recognize rent-seeking opportunities that occur during political interventions. Similarly, social entrepreneurship is thought to be an outgrowth of market and political imperfections, it emerges as entrepreneurs seek to improve on market outcomes through means other than government intervention.

Wagner suggests an alternative to the additive framework: Entangled Political Economy (Wagner 2009, 2016). One of the distinguishing features of Entangled Political Economy is the placement of political actors within the same sphere of activity as market actors. While the additive vision focuses on the impact of a polity on the economy, the entangled approach focuses on the emergence of a network of bidirectional interactions. From the perspective of Entangled Political Economy, all entrepreneurial activity occurs in the same space.

I open the paper with an overview of the ends-based taxonomy and its relationship to the additive political economy. Then I take an in-depth look at how entrepreneurship unfolds in the Entangled Political Economy. The approach of Entangled Political Economy makes it impossible to adopt the ends-based taxonomy. Instead, it distinguishes between enterprises that are supported by voluntary investors and those that are supported by involuntary investors, i.e. taxpayers. This distinction is meaningful because projects supported by voluntary investors are different from those that are supported by involuntary investors, in a number of ways. By following Wagner's distinction between voluntary and involuntary investors, I trace several significant differences between the two forms of entrepreneurship. I conclude that instead of focusing on the ends, a taxonomy of entrepreneurship should, in line with Wagner's framework of Entangled Political Economy, focus on the means, in particular, on whether the resources organized to support the venture were obtained through cooperation or coercion.

2 Ends-Based Taxonomy

Entrepreneurship scholarship is a growth industry (Elkjaer 1991; Venkataraman 1997). In 1987 an Entrepreneurship Division was added to the Academy of Management and now entrepreneurship has its own code (L26) in the Journal of Economic Literature classification (Foss and Klein 2012). As surveys of the entrepreneurship literature indicate, entrepreneurship used to feature prominently in economic literature before disappearing almost completely from economic radars in the first half of the twentieth century. The origins of the entrepreneurship literature can be traced back to Richard Cantillon's 1755 distinction between entrepreneur, employee, and landowner (Cantillon 2015).

While this long history of the entrepreneurship literature has not yielded a common definition of the term, the majority of the dominant approaches in this literature share a number of common characteristics (Podemska-Mikluch 2019). In most cases entrepreneurs are portrayed as agents of change, operating in the world of incomplete and dispersed knowledge, and facing uncertainty about the future. Scholars differ on how entrepreneurs overcome these challenges, with major approaches focusing on (1) alertness to previously unnoticed profit opportunities (Kirzner 1973) (2) creativity and leadership (Schumpeter 2008, 2013; Shackle 1972), (3) entrepreneurial judgement (Casson 1982; Foss and Klein 2012; Knight 2012), (4) experimentation akin to scientific hypothesis testing (Harper 1996) and (5) effectuation (Sarasvathy 2008).

Most entrepreneurship scholars focus on conventional entrepreneurship, that is entrepreneurship thought to occur in the institutional setting of well-defined private property rights and voluntary contracts, motivated by profit-seeking. In recent years, social and political entrepreneurship started to receive more attention.

What is social entrepreneurship? There is no shortage of definitions. Unfortunately, most of the definitions found in the literature are ambiguous and are based on concepts that themselves need further exploration. In fact, of the 37 definitions of social entrepreneurship gathered in Dacin, Dacin, and Matear, 31 explicitly refer to social values, social mission, and social problems (Dacin et al. 2010). Of course, concepts such as social values or social mission do not have clear, agreed-upon definitions, and can be interpreted very differently by different scholars and practitioners. In fact, many would argue that these concepts are meaningless as only individuals have values, missions, and problems. Only individuals act, societies do not act (Mises 1981). And since it is impossible to aggregate values and missions across individuals, there is no point of speaking about social values or social missions – just like traffic is not a giant car, many other collective structures display very different behavior from the elements that compose them (Resnick 1997). In any case, entrepreneurship scholars do seem to agree that the focus of social entrepreneurship is primarily on promoting some ambiguous notion of social value and social development as opposed to economic value (Mair and Marti 2006).

Political, or public, entrepreneurship is a term usually used to describe entrepreneurs who seek to benefit from influencing the political process. Political entrepreneurs are attracted by the prospect of reallocating slack budgetary resources and are more likely to be found in the presence of collective action problems (Schneider and Teske 1992). According to Baumol, political entrepreneurship emerges when an institutional environment renders pay-offs to unproductive or destructive activities higher than pay-offs to productive entrepreneurial activities (Baumol 1990). Another popular term for political entrepreneurship is rent-seeking, the concept originated by Gordon Tullock and labeled by Anne Krueger (Krueger 1974; Tullock 1967).

The distinction between conventional, social, and political entrepreneurship is embedded in the additive vision of political economy. These categories are closely related to the mainstream understanding of political economy which treats politics and markets as separate spheres of activity. That approach suggests that due to their many imperfections, markets must be subject to intervention by the government. Yet, the government is not immune to failure, so the fallible nature of government gives rise to political entrepreneurship and to the pursuit of rents. In that scheme of thought, social entrepreneurship is presented as an alternative to government interventions.

This implicit ends-based taxonomy suggests that entrepreneurship comes in different forms depending on the goals pursued by the entrepreneur. So that market entrepreneurs, in the pursuit of profits, are supposedly quite distinct from the social entrepreneurs who act in the pursuit of societal wellbeing. However, when actual entrepreneurial activity is considered, distinguishing between social and conventional entrepreneurship is close to impossible. After carefully reviewing the literature, Dacin et al. (2010) conclude that for profit enterprises are not distinguishable from social enterprises and vice versa.

Often, to succeed in the market, entrepreneurs might need to advance institutional change to help create the very markets they wish to take part in. As explored by Kuchař, in order to ensure the adoption of innovations, entrepreneurs must often ensure that the new practice become socially tolerated and legally recognized (Kuchař 2016). Kuchař uses the emergence of surrogate motherhood market to illustrate how entrepreneurs drive institutional changes by challenging existing institutional legal ordering and common interpretations of social phenomena. As Kuchař notes, sometimes the social and institutional aspects of entrepreneurship might appear to be disconnected; but it is often the case that entrepreneurs must contribute purposefully to the change of beliefs, habits, and institutions in order to translate their ideas into reality and make others take part in their projects.

Kuchař's argument relates to a recognition of two-tiers of entrepreneurship made by Leeson and Boettke (2009). The authors make a distinction between productive entrepreneurship that occurs within an existing institutional framework and protective entrepreneurship that seeks to bring about institutional change. The former focuses on new technologies and products that improve productivity and increase consumer satisfaction. The latter focuses on entrepreneurs who, in the absence of well-functioning government, seek to restrict predation by developing private protection technologies. When successful, protective entrepreneurship improves the institutional environment so that it becomes more conducive to productive entrepreneurship. Protective entrepreneurship is more prominent in developing countries characterized by weaker public protection technologies. The authors recognize significant limitations of protective entrepreneurship, for example, its inability to protect against state predation.

Existence of protective entrepreneurship suggests that entrepreneurship oriented at institutional and public policy changes can occur outside of rent-seeking. To foster these changes, entrepreneurs might employ a wide range of strategies: they might engage in public relation campaigns, they might encourage customers to demand regulatory change, they might publish op-eds and other persuasive pieces. Some of these methods were employed by Uber and Lyft in the effort to make ride-sharing a new legal category, overcoming the constraints of the taxicab and black car regulation (Stone 2017).

As a side note, it might be worth mentioning that the ends-based taxonomy also hides the social impact of market entrepreneurship. For example, the creation of scheduled part-time work and the consumer durable goods revolution accelerated the liberation of women from the home and their increased labor force participation (Goldin 2006; Greenwood et al. 2005; Horwitz 2015). The inventors of refrigerators and washing machines were market entrepreneurs but they sure contributed to social change. Skype, a for-profit enterprise, supports the transformation of family networks into transnational ones (Bacigalupe and Cámara 2012). There are many more examples of for-profit enterprises that enable social change. In fact, it might be worth asking: when is entrepreneurship not social?

Moreover, the separation of social entrepreneurship from profit-oriented entrepreneurship can imply that profit seeking is not a dignified activity. Following this approach, entrepreneurs get divided into either greedy or altruistic, depending on the ends they seem to pursue. As a result, and by accepting the vision of for profit entrepreneurship as separate from social entrepreneurship, scholars might be contributing to the growth of the anti-business, anti-capitalist narrative that Schumpeter feared would be produced by the success of capitalist societies (Schumpeter 2013).

3 Entrepreneurship in the Entangled Political Economy

Pointing out the many shortcomings of the additive approach to political economy, Wagner suggests an alternative framework: Entangled Political Economy (Wagner 2009, 2016). The key distinguishing feature of the Entangled Political Economy is its catallactic orientation - analytical focus is placed on societal interactions, and not on the efficiency of resource allocation as is the case within the additive approach. From the perspective of Entangled Political Economy, all actions within the system of political economy are presumed to have transactional character. This transactional character stems from the scale and complexity of society, as captured by the network-like depiction of the system that Wagner suggests. Within the network of Entangled Political Economy, each node represents either a person, an enterprise, or an agency and they all interact on the same plane. Approaching society as a network of connections facilitates the placement of dispersed knowledge at the forefront of analysis (Hayek 1937, 1945). Wagner also notes the creative nature of the system of political economy, contrasting it to the mechanical systems, a distinction originally made by Bertalanffy (1968).

All Entangled Political Economy explorations start with the recognition of economizing action (Wagner 2016 p. 85). As Wagner notes, to claim otherwise would be nonsensical. That is, all human action involves selection and pursuit of goals while economizing on means. While all human action takes on the same form, it differs in substance. The goals individuals choose to pursue are diverse and can have either biological or societal origins. However, as Wagner argues, there is little reason to pay attention to the particular goals individuals seek to pursue or why they seek these particular goals. All we need to know is that people act in the pursuit of diverse goals and that they want to be effective in what they do.

Analyzing entrepreneurship without paying much attention to the exact goals pursued by entrepreneurs might seem like a handicap at first. But it actually has significant analytical benefits. For one, it helps us escape the illusionary separation of profits, rents, and societal well-being as key forces that motivate entrepreneurs. Rather, we can proceed knowing that there are diverse motivations for entrepreneurial activity and that they often overlap. Some of them might fall into one or more of the three categories and some might be completely novel and unexpected. In any case, these goals are outside of the analytical interest, which means that we no longer need to struggle trying to place enterprises into one of these three categories.

Moreover, by not focusing on the ends, we actually gain a greater appreciation for the diversity of entrepreneurial pursuits. For example, this perspective might help us acknowledge that some investors are willing to accept a compensating differential – that is, they might wish to support an entrepreneur who pursues an engaging vision, even if this vision comes with the expectation of lower financial returns. As many case studies illustrate, it is surely possible to build a successful commercial organization that along with some financial returns also offers other benefits to its investors, i.e. participation in social change or commitment to protecting the natural environment. In fact, some investors might only care about non-financial returns, that is clearly the case with countless crowdfunding campaigns and charitable organizations. Other investors might only care about financial returns and nothing else. There is room for a great diversity of entrepreneurial pursuits within the economy. And just like there are different products offered in the market, investor returns can also come in numerous forms. What matters for our discussion is the fact that as long as the relationship between the entrepreneur and the investor is voluntary, the exact form of offered returns is not of great relevance.

Within the Entangled Political Economy, the entrepreneurial process can be depicted as a creation of new nodes in the network. Successful enterprises find support by forging connections with the existing nodes. In the process they might render some of the existing nodes and connections obsolete. Enterprises that fail to forge and maintain connections perish. Conventional connections between entrepreneurs and investors, such as those described in the previous paragraph, are dyadic - they take on the form of voluntary exchange (Podemska-Mikluch and Wagner 2013). However, not all enterprises can get support from voluntary investors. Some ideas simply do not offer enough in terms of financial returns or other benefits to attract voluntary investors. For example, Twin Cities' Metropolitan Council would be very unlikely to successfully pitch its Light Rail extension projects on Shark Tank or even on Kickstarter. And yet, the construction of the Southwest LRT is already underway. How is it possible without investor support? In case of the Twin Cities Southwest LRT project, the $2 billion bill is to be paid by the state and federal governments, or to be more precise, by taxpayers.

Wagner refers to taxpayers, and other unwilling supporters of such enterprises, as forced investors. Forced investors are coerced to support the political enterprise through changes in regulatory or fiscal policy. There are endless examples of regulatory policies that accomplish this goal, i.e. increased safety standards that benefit incumbent firms, discourage entry of competitors, and raise prices. Subsidies are an even more direct form of generating returns for the de facto owners of the enterprise, at the expense of forced investors. The cause of the worsening in the terms of trade is not always easy to identify, hence, forced investors are often ignorant of the support they provide. Involvement of forced investors changes voluntary dyads into triads. Within the triads, at least one of connections is coerced (Podemska-Mikluch and Wagner 2013).

We can make analytically meaningful distinction between two types of enterprises based on the source from which they obtain their means: those that can survive without forced investors and those that cannot. The distinction is crucial because projects supported by voluntary investors are very different from those that are supported by involuntary investors.

For one, enterprises supported by forced investors are unlikely to survive in open competition with market offerings. As I explore elsewhere, new methods of hormonal contraception delivery serve as a great example (Podemska-Mikluch 2018). When the proponents of contraceptive research and development recognized the lack of market demand for these new offerings, they turned to the government for support. It came in the form of insurance mandates (first state then federal) that require insurance plans to fully cover all forms of contraception. Without the mandates, the new, patented offerings would not be able to compete with the generic, inexpensive, and widely available pills.

It is worth noting that the adoption of contraceptive mandates was supported by the rhetoric of gender equality and reproductive justice. Combined with the religious freedom debate that emerged at that time, rhetoric successfully hid from view the redistributive aspects of the promoted policies, in particular, the expected payoffs to the pharmaceutical manufacturers. To this day, contraceptive mandates are viewed more as a successful case of social entrepreneurship than an effort to secure forced investors for otherwise unsustainable undertaking. Wagner refers to the deployment of rhetoric as a shell game, an effort to misdirect observer's attention away from where the action is truly located (Wagner 2016). Similarly, in the case of Grameen Bank, the social entrepreneurship rhetoric highlighted the benefits of microcredit, while hiding the low effectiveness of the program, despite the fact that founders were successful in obtaining generous contributions not only from donor organizations but also from governments (Schreiner 2003).

Second, access to forced investors isolates entrepreneurs from creative destruction. In fact, the apparent failure of a particular entrepreneurial venture often spurs arguments for increased financial support rather than arguments for closing up shop. Public schools are an excellent and prominent example of this – low scores on standardized tests do not result in soul searching among the providers but almost automatically lead to calls for increased school funding (Moskowitz 2017). This happens because politically-supported enterprises are not accountable to investors. Their success does not depend on the value of the enterprise but on their ability to maintain access to forced investors.

Consequently, the presence of nodes that control access to forced investors strengthens the entrenchment of the elites. In the institutional setting of contracts and private property, market success and the wealth that follows attract competition. As well-illustrated by Ludwig Lachman:

> Market competition limits concentration of wealth. It encourages the circulation of the elites. The owners of wealth, are like the guests at a hotel or the passengers in a train: They are always there but are never for long the same people. (Lachmann 2008)

This happens because under the rules of private property, no particular node in the network is necessary for success of new nodes. When new enterprises are formed, they can seek support from a variety of diverse and voluntary sources. Refusal from one investor only means that the entrepreneur must seek support somewhere else. As the connections to voluntary investors are formed, the network expands. In the process, some of the existing nodes and connections might be eroded or replaced. What is most crucial for our analysis is the fact that securing support from any particular voluntary investor is not necessary for success and therefore the process does not favor any particular nodes in the network. Because of that, the process of network expansion unfolds in a random, scalable manner (Barabási 2002; Wagner 2016). That is, growth of the network does not change the qualities of the network. In contrast, access to forced investors is closely controlled. To gain it, entrepreneurs must engage in closed competition. In the process of building enterprises that rely on support of forced investors, entrepreneurs must establish connections to specific nodes. As the competition over access to forced investors unfolds, the influence of these particular nodes grows. This results in a network that is not scalable and random, in this case, growth in the number of connections changes the nature of the network.

4 Conclusions

From the perspective of Entangled Political Economy, political, social, and market changes describe different aspects of the same emergent process. Market activity does not occur in a vacuum - to capture market profits, entrepreneurs need to invest significant effort in advancing institutional, political, and regulatory changes (Kuchař 2016; Leeson and Boettke 2009; Stone 2017). By giving up the false sense of separation between politics and markets, EPE highlights the challenges involved in meaningfully segregating entrepreneurship into the popular, widely accepted, categories. EPE also suggests that to understand the true role of various enterprises the focus needs to be on their activities, in particular, on how they go about securing investor support. Pronounced goals, and the aspirations of the involved entrepreneurs, are best left out of the analysis. Such statements might be an honest pronouncement of their purpose and mission but might also be a shell game (Wagner 2016). Hence, instead of focusing on the ends, the taxonomy of entrepreneurship needs to focus on means, in particular, on whether the resources organized to support the venture originate from voluntary or from forced investors.

References

Bacigalupe, G., & Cámara, M. (2012). Transnational families and social technologies: Reassessing immigration psychology. *Journal of Ethnic and Migration Studies, 38*(9), 1425–1438. https://doi.org/10.1080/1369183X.2012.698211.

Barabási, A. L. (2002). *Linked: The new science of networks*. Cambridge: Perseus Publishing.

Baumol, W. J. (1990). Entrepreneurship: Productive, unproductive, and destructive. *Journal of Political Economy, 98*(5), 893–921.

Bertalanffy, L. V. (1968). *General system theory*. New York: George Braziller.

Cantillon, R. (2015). *Essay on the nature of trade in general*. Indianapolis: Liberty Fund.

Casson, M. (1982). *The entrepreneur: An economic theory*. Totowa: Barnes and Noble Books.

Dacin, P. A., Dacin, M. T., & Matear, M. (2010). Social entrepreneurship: Why we Don't need a new theory and how we move forward from here. *Academy of Management Perspectives, 24*(3), 37–57. https://doi.org/10.5465/amp.24.3.37.

Elkjaer, J. R. (1991). The entrepreneur in economic theory. An example of the development and influence of a concept. *Hist Eur Ideas, 13*(6), 805–815.

Foss, N. J., & Klein, P. G. (2012). *Organizing entrepreneurial judgment: A new approach to the firm*. Cambridge: Cambridge University Press.

Goldin, C. (2006). The quiet revolution that transformed Women's employment, education, and family. *The American Economic Review, 96*(2), 1–21.

Greenwood, J., Seshadri, A., & Yorukoglu, M. (2005). Engines of Liberation. *The Review of Economic Studies, 72*(1), 109–133. https://doi.org/10.1111/0034-6527.00326.

Harper, D. A. (1996). *Entrepreneurship and the market process: An enquiry into the growth of knowledge*. London: Routledge.

Hayek, F. A. (1937). Economics and knowledge. *Economica, 4*(13), 33–54.

Hayek, F. A. (1945). The use of knowledge in society. *The American Economic Review, 35*(4), 519–530.

Horwitz, S. (2015). *Hayek's modern family: Classical liberalism and the evolution of social institutions*. New York: Palgrave Macmillan.

Kirzner, I. M. (1973). *Competition and entrepreneurship*. Chicago: The University of Chicago Press.

Klein, P. G., Mahoney, J. T., McGahan, A. M., & Pitelis, C. N. (2010). Toward a theory of public entrepreneurship. *European Management Review, 7*(1), 1–15. https://doi.org/10.1057/emr.2010.1.

Knight, F. H. (2012). *Risk, uncertainty and profit*. Mineola: Dover Publications.

Krueger, A. O. (1974). The political economy of the rent-seeking society. *The American Economic Review, 64*(3), 291–303.

Kuchař, P. (2016). Entrepreneurship and institutional change. *Journal of Evolutionary Economics, 26*(2), 349–379. https://doi.org/10.1007/s00191-015-0433-5.

Lachmann, L. (2008). The market economy and the distribution of wealth. In M. Sennholz (Ed.), *On freedom and free Enterprise: Essays in honor of Ludwig Von Mises* (pp. 175–187). Auburn: Ludwig von Mises Institute.

Leeson, P. T., & Boettke, P. J. (2009). Two-tiered entrepreneurship and economic development. *International Review of Law and Economics, 29*(3), 252–259. https://doi.org/10.1016/j.irle.2009.02.005.

Mair, J., & Marti, I. (2006). Social entrepreneurship research: A source of explanation, prediction, and delight. *Journal of World Business, 41*(1), 36–44.

Mises, L. V. (1981). *Socialism: An economic and sociological analysis*. Indianapolis: Liberty Fund.

Moskowitz, E. (2017). *The education of Eva Moskowitz: A memoir*. New York: HarperCollins.

Podemska-Mikluch, M. (2018). Contraception without romance: The entangled political economy of state and Federal Contraceptive Insurance Mandates. In R. E. Wagner (Ed.), *James M Buchanan: A theorist of political economy and social philosophy* (pp. 263–290). London: Palgrave Macmillan. https://doi.org/10.1007/978-3-030-03080-3_13.

Podemska-Mikluch, M. (2019). Entrepreneurship. In A. Marciano & G. B. Ramello (Eds.), *Encyclopedia of law and economics*. New York: Springer.

Podemska-Mikluch, M., & Wagner, R. E. (2013). Dyads, triads, and the theory of exchange: Between liberty and coercion. *The Review of Austrian Economics, 26*, 171–182. https://doi.org/10.1007/s11138-012-0180-x.

Resnick, M. (1997). *Turtles, termites, and traffic jams: Explorations in massively parallel microworlds*. Cambridge: MIT Press.

Sarasvathy, S. D. (2008). *Effectuation: Elements of entrepreneurial expertise*. Cheltenham: Edward Elgar Publishing.

Schneider, M., & Teske, P. (1992). Toward a theory of the political entrepreneur: Evidence from local government. *The American Political Science Review, 86*(3), 737–747.

Schreiner, M. (2003). A cost-effectiveness analysis of the Grameen bank of Bangladesh. *Development and Policy Review, 21*(3), 357–382. https://doi.org/10.1111/1467-7679.00215.

Schumpeter, J. A. (2008). *The theory of economic development: An inquiry into profits, capital, credit, interest, and the business cycle*. New Brunswick: Transaction Publishers.

Schumpeter, J. A. (2013). *Capitalism, socialism, and democracy*. London: Routledge.

Shackle, G. L. S. (1972). *Epistemics and economics: A critique of economic doctrines*. Cambridge: Cambridge University Press.

Stone, B. (2017). *The upstarts: How uber, Airbnb, and the killer companies of the new Silicon Valley are changing the world*. New York: Little, Brown and Company.

Tullock, G. (1967). The welfare costs of tariffs, monopolies, and theft. *Economic Inquiry, 5*(3), 224–232.

Venkataraman, S. (1997). The distinctive domain of entrepreneurship research. *Adv Entrep Firm Emergence Growth, 3*, 119–138.

Wagner, R. E. (2009). Property, state, and entangled political economy. In W. Schafer, A. Schneider, & T. Thomas (Eds.), *Markets and politics: Insights from a political economy perspective* (pp. 37–49). Marburg: Metropolis.

Wagner, R. E. (2016). *Politics as a peculiar business: Public choice in a system of entangled political economy*. Cheltenham: Edward Elgar.

From Taciturn to Talkative Political Economy

Adam Martin

Abstract Deirdre McCloskey challenges economists to take talk seriously. Public choice economics, like most economics, typically assigns only a small role to various forms of talk between individuals. By contrast, throughout Richard Wagner's oeuvre, there is an undercurrent of talk about talk. This essay argues that talk matters because of two keep assumptions in Wagner's approach to public choice. First, talk matters to the extent that individuals are ignorant. There are different forms of ignorance in economic theory which allow talk to communicate different sorts of information. Knightian uncertainty, however, also opens up the possibility that talk can do more. Second, talk matters when individuals have tuistic motivations. When individuals are moved to act based on the actions and judgments of others, talk becomes motivating as well as informative. I illustrate the power of talk in Wagner's approach by examining the classic arguments put forward in *Democracy in Deficit*.

Keywords Bounded rationality · Deliberation · Talk · Uncertainty

1 Introduction

Wagner's World is home to a number of concepts absent from most scholarship in political economy: emergence, entanglement, parasitical pricing, elections as theater, non-logical action, deep heterogeneity, and scale-free relationships, to name just a few. Wagner often meditates upon these concepts in his writing, moving from one to another. They are clearly interconnected. Accepting any one as important or helpful is liking knocking over one domino in the intricate chain of propositions that make up more typical approaches to political economy. Other propositions, including those that were only implicit, soon fall as well. The myriad ways in which these assumptions and arguments rest upon one another are amenable primarily to book-

Thanks to Dave Hebert and Diana Thomas for organizing this symposium, to Justin Callais for research assistance, to Deirdre McCloskey for helpful feedback, and to Richard Wagner for years of inspiring mentorship.

A. Martin (✉)
Texas Tech University, Lubbock, TX, USA
e-mail: Adam.martin@ttu.edu

D. J. Hebert, D. W. Thomas (eds.), *Emergence, Entanglement, and Political Economy*, Studies in Public Choice 38, https://doi.org/10.1007/978-3-030-56088-1_6

length treatments, which Wagner has spent decades churning out in rapid succession. Read them all.

This chapter aims to identify one more domino that Wagner's work knocks on: talk. Economists since Adam Smith have made a great deal of the fact that human beings—perhaps uniquely among species on this planet—trade with one another. Wagner's work stands as part of this tradition, most notably embodied in the work of his mentor and collaborator James Buchanan (1964). But language is also distinctively human. Talk accompanies virtually every form of human activity, including trade. Smith seems to have seen this connection as well: "Nobody ever saw one animal by its gestures and natural cries signify to another, this is mine, that yours; I am willing to give this for that" (Smith 1776, Book I, Ch. 2). Yet it is largely absent from most work in political economy. Is that absence justified? It may be. Models are not meant to capture every facet of reality. But we will not know what talk can do unless we identify what makes it impotent in most economic and public choice models.

Economists such as Deirdre McCloskey (McCloskey and Klamer 1995; McCloskey 2010, Ch. 41) and Bart Wilson (2018) have argued that economists as a whole should pay more attention to language. The question of this essay is thus: what would it take for a theory of talk to take hold in *political economy*? In particular, the role of talk hinges on two key assumptions in economic theory.[1] What sorts of ignorance do agents confront? And are their motivations tuistic or strictly self-regarding? Wagner's agents, I argue, confront the relevant sorts of ignorance and have the relevant sorts of motivations. I illustrate this point by highlighting all the ways that talk matters in Buchanan and Wagner's classic *Democracy in Deficit.* Talk matters in Wagner's World in a way that it cannot in other visions of political economy.

2 Communicative to Creative

Knight (1960, p. 73) famously argues that, under competitive conditions, individuals treat one another like vending machines. "Yours for $1.50." This is the extent of communication in most economic models. In a world where there are only prices and quantities, there is not much else to say. The same is true of many economic models of politics. "Yours for a 2% higher lump sum tax." Median vote wins. Sometimes, there's even less talk than this: voters observe outcomes like GDP growth and vote accordingly. There is nothing in principle wrong with such models. Quite a lot can be learned, I posit, by treating politics like a collective vending machine, especially when we distinguish who feeds the machine from who divides up the treats that issue forth. Most public choice models of such a collective vending

[1] I do not claim that these are necessary conditions for talk to matter. They are sufficient, even if they are not exhaustive.

machine would be focused on the set of possible equilibrium outcomes, or, in this case, the minimum winning cola-lition.

But Knight was thinking in terms of perfect competition, in which agents were basically perfectly informed. Allowing for incomplete information gives talk a wider field of play. Imperfectly informed agents have more reasons to chat. Knight for instance, identifies the economic function of managers with imperfect information (Knight 1921, Ch. 10). Managers monitor so that they can coordinate, command, and cajole subordinates. Information is costly, and sometimes talk is the cheapest way to economize on those costs. Similarly, when we add incomplete information to politics, talk matters more. Consumers of collective goods—if their own votes are unlikely to affect which goods are provided—might have little incentive to pay attention to their quality or which candidate provided them. Political parties become intelligible, bundling sets of policies in order to minimize the cognitive burden on voters. Candidates also have to try to get their attention. Political advertising enters the scene, involving quite a lot of talk indeed. And advertising is costly. Fortunately (for the candidates), an ignorant electorate might create sufficient cover for candidates to talk with special interest groups. Already, incorporating a little bit of ignorance gives us at least a glimpse of politics as a process. The public choice theorist can not only predict where the process will end up, but identify some of the landmarks along the way. Just past the yard signs and straight on till inauguration.

The specter of special interests raises the issue of not just incomplete but asymmetrically held information. In markets, asymmetric information threatens to "unravel" potential gains from trade as potential buyers cannot assay the value of what is on offer. This elicits a wide variety of responses, in which sellers try to establish a perception of trustworthiness: branding, costly signaling, and contracting, to name a few. Contracts are harder in politics. The collective and singular nature of policy bundles makes it hard for any one participant in the policy making process to have sufficient control of the outcome. So political agents and organizations lean heavily on branding and signaling. Family members extol the virtues of candidates running for office, possibly in an attempt to demonstrate that they are not sociopaths. Simultaneously, candidates and their supporters cast aspersions on the trustworthiness of opponents. Elected legislators deliver long, physically taxing filibusters to demonstrate their commitment to certain principles. Every sort of political agent adopts rhetorical signifiers that clearly distinguish which tribe has their loyalty. Party representatives scold dissenting members who might sully the brand. None of this is to say that these speech acts are not sincere. A truly effective signal separates the committed from the opportunistic. Besley (2006) is convinced that these sorts of signals can be sufficient to make restraints on power unwise as we elect the truly virtuous.

For most public choice theory, this is it. Talk is strictly communicative, always pointing to some other variable within the model: past behavior, preferences, agent types, policy bundles, etc. Again it is worth stressing that we learn quite a bit about political behavior from such models. But one peculiarity is worth noting. Talk is largely ephemeral to such models, such that it is actually omitted. Agents simply observe variables of interest directly or, in the case of signaling models, infer variables from behavior. Some models make information transmission and reception explicit, but without calling it talk. And they are right to do so, for it would not add anything to the substance of the model. Occam's razor has removed the tongues from the inhabitants of our economic and political models.

But ignorance doesn't stop with incomplete or asymmetric information. Ellsberg (1961) introduces the helpful metaphor of drawing balls from an urn. What Knight calls risk can be thought of this way: there are six black balls and four white balls in the urn. I reach into the urn to pull a ball out. I am ignorant of the color but I know the probability distribution: a 60% chance of black, a 40% chance of white. This is the sort of ignorance in most economic and public choice models. Individuals are ignorant of the precise values of variables, but can assign reasonable probabilities. This approach to ignorance also sometimes makes its way in at the level of populations when we assume that errors are randomly distributed, leading to results like the miracle of aggregation.

Ellsberg introduces the urn to distinguish this sort of ignorance from one he is concerned about, which he dubs ambiguity. If I am operating under ambiguity, I know the urn has only black and white balls. But I do *not* know how many balls of each color are in the urn. When I reach in to grab a ball, I cannot estimate a probability distribution. These sorts of models sometimes pop up in the study of financial assets. Epstein and Wang (1994) develop this sort of a model regarding asset pricing, showing that unknown probability distributions imply the possibility of multiple equilibria even with identical underlying fundamentals.[2] What would such a model look like in public choice?

I submit that the closest analogue to Ellsberg ambiguity in modern political economy is bounded rationality. Bounded rationality can be modeled in terms of "hill climbing" (Beinhocker 2007, Ch. 9). In these models, agents occupy a point on a fitness landscape that has hills, valleys, and pits of despair. The agents are rational—they can tell up from down—but their range of vision is limited. They can only tell the slope of the incline they are on and whether they are on a peak. They cannot see the entirety of the terrain, so they have to guess what unexplored areas look like. There is the possibility that such agents end up "stuck" at a *local* rather than a global optimum, since they do not know that there are taller peaks out there. Page (2007) uses this sort of metaphor to discuss the potential benefits of cognitive diversity. Different agents may have different *mental models*, ways of projecting and exploring through the epistemic fog they confront. A team comprised of agents with a more diverse group of models often does better at finding high points than a team whose members think the same way.

Landemore (2012) and Landemore and Page (2015) apply this sort of thinking to democratic deliberation. The problems confronted in public policy are often difficult, so it is reasonable to assume that political communities frequently confront

[2] Epstein and Wang mistakenly refer to their model as one of Knightian uncertainty, but it is clear upon examination that they are really discussing ambiguity: unknown probability distributions (c.f. Langlois 1994).

ambiguity about the effects of public policies. We might know that we want the crime rate to go down or education performance to improve, but it is not obvious what the best way to move these variables is or even how to find out whether we are stuck at a local optimum. Deliberation may enable groups of individuals with diverse ideas to create better solutions to these pressing issues. Weymark (2015) argues that this application of Page's ideas has problems, but whether correct or not the application illustrates two important points for my argument.

First, individuals confronting ambiguity have something new to talk about: mental models. Mental models come into play when agents need to conjure estimates of distributions they cannot observe. This function of mental models does not come up with less severe forms of ignorance. In an ambiguous world we can talk not only about our estimates but how we got them. The second important point is that, though these models give agents something new to talk about, they do not change the fundamental nature of talk. Talk is still just communication. In Page's models (c.f. Page 2008, pp. 212–217), agents typically report the predictions of their own mental models. Everyone believes them. No one *argues* about the validity or relevance of the models themselves, and no one updates to a new model. This seems to miss an important feature of political talk. So maybe we can learn a little more by reaching into the urn one last time.

I reach into the urn. I pull out… a green ball? That can't be right. I reach in again. I pull out a hamster. This is full blown Knightian uncertainty: ignorance of possible outcomes, not just the probabilities attached to those outcomes. I do not know what is in the urn. For Knight, uncertainty elicits not just management but *entrepreneurship*. The sort of ignorance entrepreneurs confront is not *just* "how much will this product sell for?" but also, "what product should I make in the first place?" and "how should I make it?" Entrepreneurs have to imagine what is in the urn. Explained thus, Knightian uncertainty is functionally equivalent to Israel Kirzner's concept of sheer ignorance (Kirzner 1992, Langlois 1994). How do we respond to this sheer ignorance, to these unknown unknowns? Kirzner calls it perception or discovery, and Knight (1921) sometimes uses the word judgment. I prefer *imagination.* We *imagine* possibilities before we act on them. Often these possibilities are the plans that we choose between. Imagined plans form our opportunity sets. Usually, we simply imagine the same options as yesterday.

But sometimes, we imagine something new. Uncertainty and creativity are two sides of the same coin. It is easy to get caught up pondering the philosophical question of whether we are truly "creative." Kirzner (1997) insists that his metaphor of discovering opportunities that are "out there" is just that, a metaphor, and that he is agnostic about whether humans are truly creative. This is surely the right approach to take for social science, since the social scientist is rarely (some might dare to say never) omniscient. Since we as students of society do not know all possible options confronting individuals, it is impossible for us to determine whether any novel phenomenon was created or only discovered. From the perspectives of the acting individuals whose behavior we wish to explain, options can be at least locally new.

If individuals are creative, I posit, there is something more for talk and language to do: they can facilitate (or impede) creativity. Consider two ways in which language—on top of its communicative function—facilitates creativity. First, language enables us to recombine ideas. Symbolic thought, as embodied in human language, allows concepts with certain referents to be mentally detached from their existing contexts. Bart Wilson (2018, pp. 14-17) offers the following example: once the mind has the concepts of a point, a shaft, and a haft, it can combine them into the design for a spear. These recombinations of concepts are at the heart of much innovation and economic growth (Weitzman 1998).

The second way in which talk aids creativity is through the use of metaphors. Metaphors enable us to transplant mental models from one context to another. A utility function is like the topography of a mountain. Open market operations are like an angel doubling the quantity of specie. Natural selection is like economizing. This also carries over the development of new goods and services. Nowhere is this more evident than computer programming, where metaphors of containers, objects, pointers, and other physical phenomena abound.

The move to uncertainty thus represents a state shift in the role of language. Just as water transitions from liquid to solid as its temperature rises from 211 to 212 degrees Fahrenheit, language transitions from communicative to communicative *and* creative as we descend from ambiguity to uncertainty. Once creativity exists, though, it works its way back up through the levels of ignorance. Creative individuals can formulate new search algorithms to more cheaply discover known unknowns. They can devise new and inventive ways of signaling—or feigning—sincerity and trustworthiness. Manipulations of symbolic thought lead to the generation of *new* mental models. And, touching on the subject matter of the next section, talk enables the generation of new social norms, legal rules, and moral principles.

Wagner's World has always been home to entrepreneurship and creativity, and thus to talk. In his first publication, a review of Mancur Olson's *Logic of Collective Action*, Wagner says that:

> Devoting sole attention to pressure groups is a version of the forest- trees paradox; particular features of the political environment are examined at the expense of fundamental essences. The particular feature is that some large-membership pressure groups exist in which the lobbying activity is a by-product of the provision of private services, while there simultaneously exists large-member latent groups that provide neither private nor lobbying services. The overlooked essence is that the political entrepreneur provides the key to understanding why certain groups receive real income increasing favors while others do not; favor-seeking activity results from the operation of democratic decision processes and not from pressure groups per se. (Wagner 1966, pp. 164-5).

This basic idea carries forward to Wagner's more recent contributions. Wagner (2007) reformulates public finance theory in terms of the complex relationships between market enterprises and political enterprises. Entrepreneurs play a central role in both establishing enterprises both in the market square and in the public square, as well as in forming various connections between them and providing "the source of propulsive energy within a society that sets in motion processes of continual transformation" (p. 75). Wagner (2010, Chs. 3-4) rejects the "closed" model of utility maximization, embracing the open-ended nature of choice, Knightian uncertainty, recombination as a source of novelty, and the central role of imagination.

3 Tuism and Talk

Talk can change our behavior by changing our knowledge. But what about our incentives or motivation? Crawford and Ostrom (1995) identify one promising channel by which talk might not only inform but also motivate when they discuss the "*grammar* of institutions" (emphasis added). They distinguish between institutions as shared strategies, norms, and rules. All of these institutional forms identify individuals, types of actions, and the conditions under which they apply. For shared strategies, this is it. They allow us to coordinate expectations. My students follow shared strategies when they sit in the same seat during every class period. Norms add "deontic operators," which explain whether an action is forbidden, permitted, or required. "*Do not* eat the cookies before dinner." "You *must* hold the door open for little old ladies." These deontic operators can transmit normative claims upon others. Finally, rules add both a deontic operator and an "or else" statement indicating the punishment for violators. Crawford and Ostrom's argument highlights an important feature of institutions and other normative influences on human conduct: they depend on symbolic thought—and thus on language—in a way that preferences do not.

Institutions are constituted by talk, and so talk can clearly motivate behavior. One possible objection to this claim is that talk here is still only communicative: it simply informs individuals of expectations and consequences. Hobbes famously defends such a view, arguing that "Covenants, without the Sword, are but Words, and of no strength to secure a man at all" (Hobbes 1650, Ch. 17). Hence the need for a sovereign. But Russel Hardin (1993) identifies the flaw in this Hobbesian response. To select a sovereign is already to solve a substantial coordination problem. If a society has the capacity to coordinate on an absolute sovereign, why not coordinate on a more restricted political constitution? More importantly, what gives individuals the ability to coordinate on such a scale if not talk? In Wagner's World, these bottom-up forces for social order occupy the foreground of analytical attention, flipping the Hobbesian question on its head: can there be (sovereign) swords without covenants?

Wagner relaxes one key assumption that allows talk to do real work in his theories: non-tuism. Wicksteed (1910, p. 180) points out that our standard models of supply and demand do not require the full-blown selfishness commonly attributed to *homo economicus*. Rather, they only suppose that individuals who are buying and selling do not directly take account of the interests of other parties to the exchange. As with Knight's vending machines, this modeling strategy is incredibly useful for explaining a wide range of behavior. I might buy toothpaste to donate to the local homeless shelter. Hardly selfish. However, I do not spontaneously offer the toothpaste-monger a higher price than what he asks for. The exchange itself is non-tuistic—I treat the merchant's interests instrumentally and vice versa—at the same time that it proceeds (partly) from altruistic motives. I take the price offered, just like a would from a vending machine, and I communicate just as much.[3]

Tuism, like ignorance, gives talk more to do. Ostrom (1993) recognizes this, identifying non-tuism as one of the key assumptions of public choice obscures the constitution of social order. The natural inclination for economists interested in such a move might be to integrate others' utility or consumption into an individual's utility function. I do not have the space to engage this approach here, though Vernon Smith and Bart Wilson (2019) argue that it is lacking. They also suggest a promising alternative: Adam Smith's theory of moral sentiments. Smith (1759) argues (a) that humans have the capacity for fellow-feeling, recognizing and responding to the emotions and sentiments of others, and (b) that we desire to receive and be worth of receiving others' affirmation of our actions and their underlying motives. Obviously there is a communicative function for talk here: talk can register approbation and disapprobation.

But moral sentiments also open up a new possibility: talk may be the medium by which we articulate and give reasons for action. In standard, non-tuistic models, preferences are the only form of motivation. Tuism opens up the possibility that there are other forms of motivation. If I commend an action on the grounds that it is charitable or brave, I am not necessarily saying "this action has a positive first derivative in your utility function." I might be appealing to standards that you hold or that I think you should hold, independent of their ability to serve your ends. "Do this because it is the right thing to do." For Smith these normative judgments formulated and expressed through talk not only affect momentary behavior, but ultimately shape our individual characters into vicious or virtuous forms. Tuistic talk not only provides momentary motivations, but also effects what sorts of people we are.

Other approaches to tuism exist as well, and may be complements or substitutes for the Smithian approach. McCloskey (2010, Ch. 41) argues that talk is often persuasive. One way to interpret this claim is that talk allows us to give one another normative reasons for acting.[4] Gaus (2012) develops a normative account of "public reason" which distinguishes between egoistic calculations on the one hand and moral reasons on the other. But though his account is itself an exercise in normative political theorizing, it points to one consistent theme from positive social science: non-maximizing behavior often plays an important role in accounting for the bottom-up formation of social institutions. Elinor Ostrom (2000) prefers the language of "willing punishers." These accounts all imply that the deontic operators explored by Crawford and Ostrom may have a distinct motivating force beyond their

[3] At least ideally. Few things are worse than a chatty toothpaste monger. Talk is not always a good thing. Hence Wagner's frequent appeal to Sartre, "Hell is other people" (Wagner 2007, p. 48).

[4] A Stigler and Becker (1977) approach to this might be to argue that talk is simply providing information about which forms of human capital to invest in. Again, I do not wish to settle any dispute about how fruitful this approach is compared to the one I am proposing. I will simply say that it should enjoy *at best* presumptive status based on the success of its predictions rather than unquestioned status because it is neat. And it is neat

informational content. They help trigger motivations such as reciprocity and commitment that are not reducible to incentives.

Language and our moral sentiments play a crucial role not only in animating systems of institutions and social morality but also in generating such systems. Just as language enables the creation of new ideas through recombining symbols, so too can it play a part in generating new rules, norms, or moral principles. This raises an important point. When I claim that moral emotions help generate order, I am not claiming that this is always a beneficent process. Perverse systems of order also rely on language and moral sentiments in order to take hold and thrive. Wagner's work pays ample heed to this possibility, exploring the sources of institutional and moral corruption. In line with de Jouvenal's (1963, Ch. 1) observation that the fundamental element of political behavior is when "A tells B to do C," Wagner recognizes that claims of authority over others have both intrinsic and consequential risks (Wagner 2007, Ch. 8).

In Wagner's World, tuism reigns. And so does talk. Wagner (2007) describes market and political activity as rooted in two different "grammars" of private ("mine and thine") vs. common ("us together") property. More recently, Wagner (2016) develops at length the importance of "non-logical" action for understanding political behavior, arguing that the operation of sentiments and passions is central to understanding such behavior. One of the central themes of *Mind, Society, and Human Action* (Wagner 2010) is the bi-directional relationship between mind and society. Social life shapes not only our beliefs but also our characters (Wagner 2007, Ch. 8), and different forms of political relationships can lead individuals to stand tall in liberty or bow down in subservience.

4 A Case Study: Democracy in Deficit

Talk matters to the story in Buchanan and Wagner's classic *Democracy in Deficit.* Unfortunately, it opens with some extremely misleading advertising. In the prefatory remarks about coauthoring with Richard Wagner, James Buchanan says:

> The analytical core of the argument in *Democracy in Deficit* is simple and straightforward. Indeed, the argument is perhaps the single most persuasive application of the elementary theory of public choice, which focuses primary attention on the incentives faced by choosers in varying social roles.

This is a partial truth. The core argument is simple: Keynesian demand management calls for running deficits when the economy is sluggish and surpluses when it is growing rapidly. But this prescription is not incentive compatible with democracy. Politicians love to promise spending and tax cuts in bad times but would be kicked out of office for cutting spending or raising taxes in good times. This sounds very much like elementary public choice, the sort of example we would give to our students when explaining exactly what public choice is. And there is a lot of this analysis in the book that looks at straightforward incentive issues.

But the core argument does not work with incentives alone. And, fortunately, the book doesn't rely only on incentives. At the most crucial moments in the text, the argument becomes one about ideas, knowledge, uncertainty and talk. Consider the argument in chapter "Political Property Rights and Entangled Political Economy", "Institutional Constraints and Political Choice." The authors know they have to confront the issue of Ricardian Equivalence. If deficits are future taxes, then the "consequences of Mr. Keynes" might be nothing more than redistributing taxes through time. In an incentives-only story, a median voter would have little reason to support politicians whose policies continue to run up chronic deficits; if they did so, it would have to be understood as intentional tax smoothing.

Buchanan and Wagner's response is, in part, to invoke the concept of "fiscal illusion." They state that "it is the *perceptions* of individuals concerning the differential effects of fiscal institutions that are relevant to potential fiscal choice" and that "different tax institutions will exert differing effects on the individual's perception of his share of the costs of public services" (p. 132). Because tax burdens *for individuals* are uncertain events in the future, the ability to run a deficit lowers the perceived cost of government spending, increasing the size and scope of government as a spontaneous outcome rather than an intentional decision by a median voter.

Throughout *Democracy in Deficit*, these knowledge issues rear their heads at key moments. We hear about individuals who have differing *theories* of how the world works, such as Keynesians, Classical economists, and public choice economists. These models are often spelled out in metaphors about prudent families, fiscal "drag," and pushing and pulling on strings. We hear about different *political norms*, such as the "old time fiscal religion" or functional finance. And we hear about the subjective perceptions of individual decision makers that may or may not conform with the underlying reality. Deficits are indeed future taxes (or inflation), but deficit financing changes how we see them. These moving pieces call to mind Vincent Ostrom's claim that the really important advances in public choice theory are "thrusts at the periphery," by which he means work that takes issues of knowledge and "epistemic choice" seriously (Ostrom 1993).

For the argument in *Democracy in Deficit* to work, it needs talk to matter. Talk is the medium through which both ideas and institutions exert influence on the world. Theories such as Keynesian demand management are formulated, debated, and spread through talk. In order to take hold and influence individuals' mental models, they have to be *discussed* in Knight's sense. What would count as good evidence for or against this idea? The Old Time Fiscal Religion is a norm that tells us: "*if* we are not in a state of war *then* balance the budget." A Keynesian fiscal constitution sends a different message.

In public choice as in all of economics, incentives are where the rubber hits the road. But ideas and institutions fuel the engine. Without changes in knowledge both across time and across institutions, the Buchanan-Wagner story lose its source of motion. Talk is the medium through which those changes take place. In an equilibrium state, by contrast, talk is superfluous. Talk would needlessly complicate an equilibrium story since incentives are already aligned. Just like Cantillon or injection effects don't matter in strictly comparative static analysis, talk doesn't matter either (c.f. Vaughn 1980).

What about the effects of Keynesianism on talk? Based on the account given in *Democracy in Deficit*, there seem to be two main effects that Keynesianism has on talk. First, talk about fiscal matters becomes talk among experts. Buchanan and Wagner describe the "presuppositions of Harvey Road," and while a simple mental model of a lone Wyrmtongue whispering in King Theoden's ear is a nice approximation of this view for some purposes, it glosses over the fact that it is a loose knit network of would-be Wyrmtongues at nice resorts that actually develop the ideas and practices that come to constitute Keynesian policy. *Democracy in Deficit* devotes two chapters to describing the process by which Keynesian ideas were diffused from the U.K. to the U.S. academy to the policy world. The Old Time Fiscal religion, folksy as it is, relied on analogies that were far more easily understood by the average citizen. A move towards fiscal issues being the purview of elite technocrats is a move away from democratic self-governance, even if it is a small one. In this sense Keynesianism might be considered incompatible not only with the incentives of institutional democracy but also with the stated ideals of normative democratic theory.

Peter Orszag, coming from a view closer to Keynes than to that of Buchanan and Wagner and in an article subtitled "why we need less democracy," makes this explicit:

> In an 1814 letter to John Taylor, John Adams wrote that "there never was a democracy yet that did not commit suicide." That may read today like an overstatement, but it is certainly true that our democracy finds itself facing a deep challenge: During my recent stint in the Obama administration as director of the Office of Management and Budget, it was clear to me that the country's political polarization was growing worse—harming Washington's ability to do the basic, necessary work of governing… In other words, radical as it sounds, we need to counter the gridlock of our political institutions by making them a bit less democratic. (Orszag 2011)

For good or for ill, certain fiscal constitutions may not be compatible with democratic deliberation. But I want to raise a more substantial concern about Keynes and talk. In Wagner's *Deficits, Debt, and Democracy* (2012), he resurrects an idea from Antonio Viti de Marco (p. 50): that deficit financing makes the fiscal commons more opaque. Because of the uncertainty of future tax burdens, the more we rely on deficit financing, the more difficult it is to grasp the tradeoffs involved in different public policy bundles. Wagner also contrasts organization according to private contracts with a fiscal commons. This distinction is important, because not only are contracts voluntary, they also embody honesty. A fiscal commons, by contrast, can run entirely on cheap talk, and deficit financing makes talk even cheaper (p. 125). So if Buchanan and Wagner are right, Keynesianism not only removed an important constraint on deficit spending, but it also removed an important constraint on dishonesty, dissembling, and other attempts to obscure reality in political discourse. Even if the Old Time Fiscal Religion relied on a false analogy, it had the virtue of imposing *some* measure of honesty in discussion of taxes and spending. A regime of normalized deficits, by contrast, involves systemic dishonesty about the distribution of benefits and future liabilities. Gaus, Gerald (2011, 496), citing Buchanan and Wicksell, raises concerns along these lines, arguing that deficit financing thus violates contractarian norms. Deficits make us dishonest.

5 Conclusion

This essay has argued that talk matters in political economy under two conditions. They are sufficient conditions, and may not be necessary ones. First, the role of talk is proportionate to the severity of ignorance that political economic agents confront. Risk, asymmetric information, ambiguity, and Knightian uncertainty each deepen the role of talk as a form of communication. However, uncertainty also introduces the possibility of creativity. In a world with creative agents, talk helps *constitute* and not merely *represent* the set of options that individuals have.

Second, I have argued that talk matters to the extent that agents are tuistic in their motivations. If we care how others think and behave, language becomes a tool of human sociality. It not only communicates judgments but helps construct them, thereby actively regulating and motivating individual conduct. This motivational role of talk further reflects back onto the internal life of individuals, making talk a tool for evaluating and shaping one's own conduct and character. Wagner's unique approach to public choice opens up both of these possibilities, giving talk a foothold in the world of political economic theory.

But perhaps we can go further. For the last 50 years, economic science has been the leading partner in the renewed dance with political science. Public choice theory was a watershed, applying models developed to explain market activity to politics. The influence has been largely, though not entirely, one-directional. But as the work of the Ostroms, Wagner, and de Jouvenal demonstrate, talk should—at least in principle—have an even more central role in political activity than economic activity. Talk is even more inseparable from collective action than it is from bilateral exchange, especially given the plasticity of human groupings. If political economists begin to take talk seriously, then, it is possible that political science could begin to lead the dance, simply because political subjects have more raw material from which to develop an analytical approach to talk. It is worth noting here that political science is, in this regard, less methodologically rigid than economics. Whether political scientists would be willing to take up this challenge and whether economists would be willing and able to respond, though, depends on one crucial factor: are we willing to live in Wagner's World?

References

Beinhocker, E. (2007). *The origin of wealth: The radical remaking of economics and what it means for business and society*. Brighton: Harvard Business Review Press.

Besley, T. (2006). *Principled agents? The political economy of good government*. Oxford: Oxford University Press.

Buchanan, J. (1964). What should economists do? *Sou Economics of Journal, 30*(3), 213–222.

Crawford, S., & Ostrom, E. (1995). A grammar of institutions. *American Political Science Review, 89*(3), 582–600.

de Jouvenel, B. (1963). *The pure theory of politics*. Cambridge: Cambridge University Press.

Ellsberg, D. (1961). Risk, ambiguity, and the savage axioms. *Quarterly Journal of Economics, 75*(4), 643–669.

Epstein, L., & Wang, T. (1994). Intertemporal asset pricing under Knightian uncertainty. *Econometrica, 62*(2), 283–322.

Gaus, G. (2011). *The order of public reason*. Cambridge: Cambridge University Press.

Gaus, G. (2012). *The order of public reason: A theory of freedom and morality in a diverse and bounded world*. Cambridge: Cambridge University Press.

Hardin, R. (1993). From power to order, from Hobbes to Hume. *Journal of Political Philosophy, 1*(1), 69–81.

Hobbes, T. [1909] (1650). Hobbes's Leviathan reprinted from edition of 1651 with an essay by the late Smith WGP. Oxford: Clarendon Press.

Kirzner, I. (1992). *The meaning of the market process: Essays in the development of modern Austrian economics*. New York: Routledge.

Kirzner, I. (1997). The Kirznerian way: An interview with Israel M. *Kirzner. Australian Economy News, 17*, 1.

Knight, F. (1921). *Risk, uncertainty, and profit*. Boston: Riverside Press.

Knight, F. (1960). *Intelligence and democratic action*. Cambrige: Harvard University Press.

Landemore, H. (2012). *Democratic reason: Politics, collective intelligence, and the rule of the many*. Princeton: Princeton University Press.

Landemore, H., & Page, S. E. (2015). Deliberation and disagreement: Problem solving, prediction, and positive dissensus. *Politics, Philosophy and Economics, 14*(3), 229–254.

Langlois, R. (1994). Risk and uncertainty. In P. Boettke (Ed.), *The Elgar companion to Austrian economics*. Northampton: Edward Elgar Publishing.

McCloskey, D. (2010). *Bourgeois dignity: Why economics can't explain the modern world*. Chicago: University of Chicago Press.

McCloskey, D., & Klamer, A. (1995). One quarter of GDP is persuasion. *American Economic Review, 85*(2), 191–195.

Orszag, P. (2011). *Too much of a good thing: Why we need less democracy*. New Republic. https://newrepublic.com/article/94940/peter-orszag-democracy

Ostrom, V. (1993). Epistemic choice and public choice. *Pub Ch, 77*(1), 163–176.

Ostrom, E. (2000). Collective action and the evolution of social norms. *Journal of Economic Perspectives, 14*(3), 137–158.

Page, S. (2007). *The difference*. Princeton: Princeton University Press.

Page, S. (2008). *The difference: How the power of diversity creates better groups, firms, schools, and societies*. Revised ed. Princeton: Princeton University Press.

Smith, A. [1985] (1759). *The theory of moral sentiments*. Carmel: Liberty Fund Inc.

Smith, A. [2009] (1776). *An inquiry into the nature and causes of the wealth of nations*. Carmel: Liberty Fund Inc.

Smith, V., & Wilson, B. (2019). *Humanomics: Moral sentiments and the wealth of nations for the twenty-first century*. Cambridge: Cambridge University Press.

Stigler, G., & Becker, G. (1977). De gustibus non est disputandum. *The American Economic Review, 67*(2), 76–90.

Vaughn, K. (1980). Does it matter that costs are subjective? *Sou Economics Journal, 46*, 702–715.

Wagner, R. (1966). Pressure groups and political entrepreneurs: A review article. *Pub Ch, 1*, 161–170.
Wagner, R. (2007). *Fiscal sociology and the theory of public finance: An exploratory essay*. Northampton: Edward Elgar Publishing.
Wagner, R. (2010). *Mind, society, and human action: Time and knowledge in a theory of social economy*. New York: Routledge.
Wagner, R. (2012). *Deficits, debt, and democracy: Wrestling with tragedy on the fiscal commons*. Northampton: Edward Elgar Publishing.
Wagner, R. (2016). *Politics as a peculiar business: Insights from a theory of entangled political economy*. Northampton: Edward Elgar Publishing.
Weitzman, M. (1998). Recombinant growth. *Quarterly Journal of Economics, 113*(2), 331–360.
Weymark, J. (2015). Cognitive diversity, binary decisions, and epistemic democracy. *Episteme, 12*(4), 497–511.
Wicksteed, P. (1910). *The common sense of political economy: Including a study of the human basis of economic law*. Whitefish: Kessinger Publishing.
Wilson, B. (2018). *The meaning of property in things* (Working paper).

Entanglement and Perverse Spontaneous Orders

Meg Patrick Tuszynski

Abstract This paper examines the evolution of spontaneous orders within Wagner's entangled political economy framework. Most examinations of how interventions affect spontaneous orders use what Wagner calls an "additive" framework of political economy. That is to say, they take as their starting point an unhampered market order, and evaluate what happens when the polity begins to encroach on the economy. Wagner, by contrast, considers polity and economy to be so intimately entwined as to be logically inseparable in many situations. This paper examines the implications for the evolution of spontaneous orders if we take entanglement as the starting point of our analysis. Few orders emerge within a pure market context, and few political actions are able to be fully centrally planned. Coupled with the fact that people are alert to opportunities to better their circumstances in all environments, this helps us better understand why some emergent orders might evolve which are considered perverse from the standpoint of those participating in those orders. This paper concludes by applying the entangled political economy framework to the case of the evolution of the public aid system in the United States. Certainly, this system is characterized by significant public ordering, but it is also the case that the ecology of relationships and enterprises that have emerged in response to the public aid system are different than what would otherwise exist.

Keywords Spontaneous order · Intervention · Entangled political economy
Entanglement · Additive political economy

JEL Codes B53 · D78 · D85 · P16

1 Introduction

The order that results from human actions and interactions is truly a wonderous thing. Individuals, acting on their own unique, local knowledge and responding to the incentives generated by the systems in which they operate are able to devise

M. P. Tuszynski (✉)
Southern Methodist University, Dallas, TX, USA
e-mail: mtuszynski@smu.edu

D. J. Hebert, D. W. Thomas (eds.), *Emergence, Entanglement, and Political Economy*,
Studies in Public Choice 38, https://doi.org/10.1007/978-3-030-56088-1_7

solutions to problems no central planner could begin to design. They are able to nimbly respond to even the smallest changes in relative prices, since they are directly affected by these changes and have the desire to constantly better their own circumstances. Indeed, Hayek describes the order that emerges within markets as a "marvel" (1945: 527). He goes on to say that he is "convinced that if it were the result of deliberate human design, and if the people guided by the price changes understood that their decisions have significance far beyond their immediate aim, [the price] mechanism would have been acclaimed as one of the greatest triumphs of the human mind" (ibid.).

In his work on spontaneous orders, Hayek continuously distinguishes between "made orders" and "grown orders" (1973: chapter 2), the former of which characterize the governmental sector, and the latter of which characterize the private sector. Indeed, much of Hayek's work can be viewed as an attempt to draw out in what ways spontaneous orders promote coordination and cooperation, and how consciously crafted orders often fail to achieve even their stated goals.

The wide body of literature which builds on Hayek's examination of the efficacy of spontaneous orders similarly draws a sharp distinction between the spontaneous order processes that characterize economic systems and the conscious direction that characterizes governmental systems. In recent work, however, Wagner draws into question the empirical usefulness of such a sharp distinction (2009, 2016). According to Wagner, frameworks which treat polity and economy as logically separable can be described as having an additive orientation toward political-economic systems. Within such frameworks, government interventions can be viewed as intruding on an otherwise relatively well-functioning market order. Interventions cause distortions in relative prices and a breakdown of the feedback mechanisms that support an efficient allocation of resources. Wagner proposes an alternative framework, which he calls entangled political economy. According to this framework, the polity and the economy are intimately intertwined such that taking about polity intervening on economy is nearly nonsensical. Polity and economy operate in the same social space. The entangled orientation towards political economy recognizes that "the presence of politics [is] ubiquitous" (Wagner 2014: 26). Political and market participants are the same people. Market transactions are imbued with political considerations, and political actions occur within a market context. There are transactions that are nearer or further away from a purely market setting, but few can be said to take place within an unhampered market.

Both additive and entangled political economy provide useful frameworks for answering different types of questions. Most existing work on spontaneous orders, however, takes place within an additive framework. This paper explores what it means to think about the evolution of order within an entangled framework. Once we recognize the fundamentally entangled nature of the political and the economic, we can also evaluate how orders can evolve that appear unbeneficial in some ways, even to those directly affected by these systems. That is to say, orders can emerge and evolve that are perverse, or undesirable from the standpoint of those participating in them. This paper follows Martin and Storr in defining a perverse emergent order as one that is "the result of human action but not human design; [but] unlike positive spontaneous orders ... cannot be said to be socially beneficial" (2008: 74). Because we live in a world characterized by various levels of mixture between the political and economic, it is not always clear whether systemic failures are due to a failure of the marketplace or a failure of the political system. This makes perverse emergent orders all the more pernicious; it is often unclear whether further political actions or a movement back toward a market order would remedy the situation.

This paper contributes to three distinct strands of literature. First, it contributes to the body of work on interventionism, which is most fully explored by Ikeda (1997, 2005), who builds on the work of both Mises (1977[1929], 1998) and Hayek (1976[1944]). This literature, however, employs an additive orientation toward political economic questions. The polity is clearly intervening in the market in these analyses. Mixed systems are thought to be inherently unsustainable, since the problems that manifest themselves in the wake of various interventions must be fixed either by more intervention or by removing the original intervention. Here, intervention is seen as government intrusion into otherwise well-working markets. This analysis also takes as its starting point (as does Ikeda) that our world is characterized by mixed systems, with some being closer to the market end of the spectrum and some being closer to the planned end of the spectrum. However, the current argument works within an entangled instead of an additive framework. This paper is, consequently, also adding to the growing literature on entangled political economy (see, for example, Horwitz and Koppl 2014). It is certainly the case that those evaluating the dynamics of mixed systems recognize that the world is characterized by significant degrees of entanglement, but that recognition is generally left in the analytical background; this paper brings it into the analytical foreground. Finally, the paper contributes to the large literature on spontaneous orders.

This argument is perhaps closest to that of Kirzner (1985), who examines the various ways in which regulations distort the otherwise orderly workings of the market process. As section three will discuss more fully, Kirzner recognizes that entrepreneurs continue to operate within regulated environments, but discovery processes that result are likely to be different in character than those that would result absent these interventions. Though Kirzner adopts an additive notion of political economy, the dynamic process he is describing parallels nicely with what I am describing here. Indeed, in many ways this paper is using the framework of Wagner's entanglement theory to probe some new dynamics of the distorted discovery processes Kirzner discusses.

The next section provides a fuller examination of how entangled political economy helps us understand the dynamics of mixed systems in ways the additive framework of existing intervention studies do not. The third section explores how perverse spontaneous orders might emerge and persist in a system characterized by significant entanglement. The fourth section evaluates how our ecology of public aid programs in the United States might adequately be characterized as a perverse emergent order. Though this system is, of course, characterized by significant amounts of political action, it has also changed the norms and characteristics of market participants, and has resulted in the evolution of an order that would likely look dramatically different absent this type of a system being in place. The final section draws implications and concludes.

2 Entangled Political Economy and the Logic of Intervention

Most examinations of the admixture between the political and the economic take as their starting point that polities and economies are two separate realms of human activity. The stated purpose of political activity, in this view, is to help "fix" those economic outcomes that are deemed to be undesirable in some way. With activities that are against a person's long-term interests, such as smoking and drinking, political actors can simply impose sin taxes to discourage these types of behaviors. When individuals, through either bad luck or bad choices, fall on hard times, political actors can redistribute income from those with more and give it to those with less. When factories produce an objectionable amount of pollutants, politicians and bureaucrats can implement regulations to discourage this sort of activity.

All three examples – taxation, redistribution, and regulation – treat economic activity and government interventions as occurring sequentially. That is to say, outcomes that some deem undesirable occur in markets at t1 and political actors impose their solutions at t2; economic actors act in the first period, and political actors work to alleviate the perceived undesirable outcomes of market activity in the second period. In this view, economy and polity are additive notions, with the locus of power known as a polity operating on the object known as economy. The studies examining the logic of intervention (see Mises 1929, 1940; Hayek 1944; Ikeda 1997, 2005) work within this additive notion of political economy. A major focus of these studies is on what happens at t3, in the post-intervention phase. Each use of a political action to "fix" the shortcomings of economic activity comes with its own set of unintended consequences. Once these unintended consequences begin to surface, if the undesirable side effects of an intervention are serious enough, those who are responsible for the intervention are faced with either repealing the intervention or enacting another intervention to alleviate the undesirable side effects of the first. If they choose the latter path, it is likely that more unintended consequences will flow from this intervention, requiring political actors to once again choose between enacting another intervention and repealing the original intervention(s).

While this is certainly an oversimplification of the very nuanced points made by scholars working in this area, this description provides us with enough information to understand that they are working within what Wagner calls an additive notion of political economy. Polity is intervening detrimentally on an otherwise well-working market order. Indeed, Ikeda defines the dynamics of intervention to be "constituted by the unintended consequences at the interface between the governmental and market processes, when the scope of government is either expanding or contracting in relation to the market" (2005: 21; emphasis mine). It is clear from statements of this type that for Ikeda, the domain of the market and the domain of the government are logically separable. Intervention, in this view, is problematic because it disrupts the otherwise orderly workings of the market system. It is also problematic because market orders and planned governmental orders have fundamentally different operating principles. Polities operate according to the principles of bureaucratic management; economic systems operate according to the principles of profit management. However, these are not easily pursued within the context of a single plan. In Mises' conception of intervention, he claims that the interventionist system must either tend toward full planning or fully free markets, since the admixture of the two is fundamentally unsustainable. However, Ikeda, noting that interventionist systems are ubiquitous, says that "instability does not imply transience any more than survival implies success" (2005: 45). Still, he does contend that mixed systems will continuously be in a state of tension, since the operating principles underlying market systems are incompatible with the operating principles underlying central planning. This will result in a series of micro- and macro-crises to try to alleviate these incompatibilities, with the size of the government sector more often growing in comparison to the market sector than the other way around.

Patrick and Wagner (2015) explore the differences between the dynamics of intervention and the dynamics of entangled political economy. While these frameworks are undoubtedly analytical cousins, the latter rejects the additive framework of the former. As Wagner (2016) explains, "[w]ith entangled political economy, prudent commercial conduct cannot be determined independently of the desires expressed by political entities; likewise, prudent political action depends on complementary commercial action" (34). Here, the analytical usefulness of the sharp dividing line between governments and markets is called into question. According to Wagner, the same people are participants in both market and government activities in different facets of their lives. "It is misleading," he says, "to speak of governmental intervention into markets because those governmental entities are themselves participants within a society's market arrangements" (2016: ix). Individuals participate in society in various ways, with no single individual able to exert any sort of systemic influence.

Within the framework of entangled political economy, the social part of "social science" occupies the foreground of analysis. This is in contrast to much of modern social science, in which the second of those words tends to predominate. Instead of focusing on the actions and interactions of individuals, much of modern social science – particularly economics – engages in representative agent type theorizing, and harnesses the tools of the scientific community for analysis. While this type of analysis is useful for answering some types of questions, minimizing the social does have its drawbacks. Entangled political economy instead pointedly focuses on human sociality and sociability. Further, it is a thoroughly ground-up approach to understanding broader macro-phenomena. Complex social orders are the result of millions of individual-level transactions. It is not just the case that order emerges through these individual-level transactions, but also that the higher-level configurations influence the incentives and norms of individual actors in a sort of self-sustaining feedback loop (Wagner 2010; Lewis 2012). "The subtext of entangled political economy," says Wagner, "focusses analytical attention on the knowledge-generating properties of different patterns of interaction among persons and entities within society" (2016: 40). Interaction, transaction, and participation are all appropriate descriptions of the driving forces behind entangled political economies.

It is important to note that entanglement is not a new phenomenon. Just looking at the U.S. context, though the size and scope of government has grown dramatically over the past 150 years, some level of entanglement has existed between political and economic actors since at least the colonial period according to Hughes (1977). If the size of the government is very small relative to the size of the economy, as it was in the colonial period, the resultant relative price distortions are likely to be minimal. The faith we have in the market to serve as an error correction device is much stronger when market actors are less able to profit through the political process. While commingling between market and political actors is unavoidable even with the smallest government, if the rents to be gained are sufficiently low, few people will be enticed to engage in rent seeking behavior. Still, any government that performs any functions beyond the most basic protective functions creates space for some private actors to attempt to gain an advantage.

Conceptually, we can separate out the features that characterize public ordering and those that characterize private ordering. The entanglement framework forces us to question whether these ideal types of orders actually exist anywhere in reality. If it is the case that some degree of entanglement characterizes most transactions and interactions, then there are at least three significant implications for spontaneous order theorizing. One, it helps us to understand that undesirable outcomes can usually not be attributed purely to pernicious market actors nor to pernicious government actors, but rather some admixture between representatives of the two groups. Two, it implies that remedies that prescribe either increased government activity or increased scope for market activity will often be misguided. Though considering the full entangled ecology of interactions is difficult, these sorts of considerations will help point the way toward more sustainable remedies for undesirable orders. Three, it helps us to understand in a more holistic way why some orders are more socially beneficial than others. This final point has particular implications for the way we think about polycentric systems. It is not simply the fact that an order is polycentric that makes it socially beneficial. Rather, beneficial outcomes result from particular constellations of public and private entities interacting within particular sets of rules.

3 Entanglement and Perverse Spontaneous Orders

Generally, analyses of spontaneous orders focus on how these orders operate in a market context. Within the market setting, spontaneous orders generally tend toward beneficial outcomes over the long term. They result from individuals pursuing their own self-interest, but are not actively designed by any individual or group of individuals. While individual actions can certainly result in outcomes that are undesirable at a point in time, the positive and negative feedback loops generally work to ensure those orders which persist are socially beneficial in some broad sense. The discipline of the profit and loss mechanism within markets, for example, provides strong incentives for errors to be corrected.

While there is a tendency to view spontaneous orders as beneficial simply due to the fact that they emerged spontaneously, many have noted that spontaneous orders can be pernicious if the conditions are right (Whitman 1998; Caldwell 2000; Angner 2004). Martin and Storr (2008) carry this idea the furthest in examining how perverse spontaneous orders might arise and persist. According to Martin and Storr, "Like language, the common law, society itself and other positive spontaneous orders, perverse emergent orders are the result of human action but not human design. But, unlike positive spontaneous orders, perverse emergent orders cannot be said to be socially beneficial" (2008: 74). Though they claim that these types of orders are common, they also acknowledge that the academic literature has paid relatively little attention to them. Leeson and Suarez (2015) provide an important caveat. They claim that some spontaneous orders that appear on their surface to be dysfunctional are actually very likely completely rational and likely socially beneficial when viewed through the appropriate lens.

Martin and Storr (2008) examine how mob behavior and negative belief systems (they use the Bahamian example of Rabbyism) fit the criteria of a spontaneous order, but nonetheless are perverse in a real sense. These both are examples of private orders. Though few orders can be classified as purely public or purely private, these orders are very close to the private end of the spectrum. However, both of the examples they use are orders that emerge in response to government activities. Consequently, we can evaluate them within the framework of entangled political economy. Certainly, this sort of entanglement is latent in the background of their analysis, but it is worth bringing to the analytical foreground in order to make sense of the relationship between entanglement and the evolution of perverse spontaneous orders.

Consider their example of social violence in more detail. "Rioters", note Martin and Storr,

> act out of anger in response to disappointments and frustrated hopes … [Riots] are, ultimately, an attempt by members of an aggrieved population to have their grievances heard and their problems redressed when all other avenues for airing their issues and seeking redress have been exhausted or appear closed off (2008: 79).

The example they use is that of the 1942 Bahamian riot that occurred when local construction workers realized they were being paid substantially less than their American counterparts for performing the same tasks. Though the American contractor employing these workers had wished to pay them more, the Bahamian government had forced their wages to be pegged to the local rate. Smaller demonstrations at the worksite had been unsuccessful, so on June 1st rioters stormed the Colonial Administration Offices and the Parliament Building on Bay Street. Like most riots, there was no central organizer or leader; the riot was rather the result of shared sentiments boiling over amongst a great many discontents. While riots may seem like they don't fit the "order" criteria of being a spontaneous order, there are generally clear rules that the rioters follow. In this example, the businesses of those considered somewhat responsible for the labor troubles were subject to the rioters' violence, while the businesses of those who were not responsible were avoided. Indeed, rioters actively signaled to one another which buildings to leave unharmed. Like most riots, there was a great deal of violence, but there was also a great deal of order to the operations.

Neither the rioters themselves nor the targets of their violence could claim this outcome was socially beneficial, but this episode nonetheless meets the criteria of being an emergent order. Importantly, however, this episode would not have occurred had there not been a strong level of entanglement between the American company and the Bahamian government. Though the American company actively wished to pay the Bahamian workers more money for their services, they knew they would be unable to operate on the islands at all if they didn't acquiesce to the government's demands. While many would look at this episode and find fault with the American company for paying Bahamian and American workers disproportionate wages, the problem in reality stemmed from the fact that the Bahamian government injected itself into this labor exchange process. The spontaneously generated mob violence emerged in response to the entanglement between the market and the government. Consequently, those who find fault with the government and those who find fault with the market in this case are both right in some sense. The order that emerged did not take place in a pure market context, nor was it the response to pure central planning, but rather the result of the intimate relationship between the economic and political actors.

To use a more recent example, consider President Bush's comments about the causes of the 2008 financial crisis. It is worth quoting his "Speech to the Nation on the Economic Crisis" at some length:

I'm a strong believer in free enterprise, so my natural instinct is to oppose government intervention. I believe companies that make bad decisions should be allowed to go out of business. Under normal circumstances, I would have followed this course. But these are not normal circumstances. The market is not functioning properly. There has been a widespread loss of confidence, and major sectors of America's financial system are at risk of shutting down. The government's top economic experts warn that, without immediate action by Congress, America could slip into a financial panic and a distressing scenario would unfold (New York Times 2008; italics are mine).

Though the Republican Party has traditionally been the party that is most supportive of capitalist activity, in this case Bush concluded that market failures had led to the current financial calamities. In their examination of the crisis, however, Smith et al. (2011) conclude that the systemic failures during this episode are better attributed to the substantial levels of entanglement that existed between the government and the banking system. The emergence of the crisis was not due solely to missteps by financial institutions, nor to misguided government policies. Rather, the perverse order that characterized the 2008 financial crisis emerged within a system characterized by substantial entanglement. It is difficult to determine whether the problems were primarily due to misguided government policy or missteps on the part of those working in the financial sector; in a real sense, the blame lies simultaneously with both. The entanglement that characterized this sector created an environment that cultivated a perverse order.

Not only does the entanglement framework help provide ex-post explanations of phenomena, but it also helps explain the dynamics of spontaneous orders that emerge in the context of this type of entanglement. Up to this point, the focus has been on the former. However, the order that emerges in systems characterized by substantial amounts of entanglement is fundamentally different from the types of order that would emerge in a pure market context. Individuals respond to incentives, and the incentives are structured by the institutional framework within which they find themselves. Markets provide the institutional framework for largely beneficial types of orders to emerge, since the discipline of the profit and loss mechanism provides strong feedback for market participants. In both of the above cases, however, entanglement meant that market signals were not reliable benchmarks for guiding action. In the case of the financial crisis in particular, banks were incentivized to behave in ways they would not have behaved absent government involvement in their activities. In a very real sense, the order that existed in the banking industry evolved over time as a result of continuously changing relationships between the individual banks and the government actors with whom they interacted.

If entanglement characterizes much of social reality, then saying that spontaneous orders that emerge within a market context tend to have beneficial characteristics is making a claim about only a small subset of the orders which actually exist. Certainly prices provide strong feedback in a market system; but most prices are distorted to some extent by political considerations. Those orders which emerge in contexts where entanglement is less pervasive will be more likely to be beneficial over the long run, since market dynamics will work to eliminate errors and promote mutually beneficial outcomes. Those which emerge in settings of more substantial entanglement run the risk of having undesirable characteristics, since market dynamics will not be able to work as effectively.

Individuals continually work to improve their situation. As Mandeville contends, private vices may result in public benefits at the system level if the institutional conditions are right (1714). If individuals are operating on the basis of distorted relative price information, however, it is not at all clear that the characteristics of the resulting system will be beneficial. Further, acting on distorted information may itself result in further systemic distortions, and so on ad infinitum. In this way, the dynamics of emergent order in an entangled framework can result in increasing perversities.

This argument is similar to that of Kirzner (1985), who argued that interventions which attempt to impose regulatory corrections on market processes can result in not only unanticipated consequences, but also consequences that may be largely undesirable from a social standpoint. While he is working within an additive framework, his analysis can readily be adapted to an entangled framework. According to Kirzner, government intrusions into the otherwise orderly workings of the marketplace can result in four different types of processes. The first of these he calls the "undiscovered discovery process", in which regulators lack faith in the market's abilities, and systematically consider interventions to be improvements over an alternative market process. The second he calls the "unsimulated discovery process", which refers to the lack of a price-like mechanism in the regulatory system, therefore no similarly beneficial way for regulators to discover the sorts of information they need. The third is the "stifled discovery process", in which price distortions created by regulation block beneficial market processes that might have otherwise emerged. Finally, he details the "wholly superfluous discovery process", in which individuals responding to the incentives of the regulatory environment set in motion a sequence of entrepreneurial activities that would not have occurred absent the regulations.

If, with Kirzner, we consider these "perils of regulation" to take place within the context of an additive orientation toward political economy, there is some hope that a swinging of the pendulum away from intervention and back toward markets might eradicate – or at least alleviate – these problematic discovery processes. If, however, we consider economy and polity to be fundamentally entangled, then we have reason to think these types of discovery processes will be pervasive.

4 Ecology of Public Aid Enterprises in the U.S.

The previous sections sketched a framework for understanding the emergence and evolution of a perverse spontaneous order. This section focuses on a particular type of order, one which is a paradigmatic example of a perverse emergent order: the social order surrounding public assistance in the United States. As Hayek recognized, it is important to clearly demarcate the parameters of the order under examination, since orders at a lower level are themselves part of a larger social order. According to Hayek, "the family, the farm, the plant, the firm, the corporation and the various associations, and all the public institutions including government, are organizations which in turn are integrated into a more comprehensive spontaneous order" (1973, 46). I am interested here in examining only a subset of the order of society. Certainly, the perversity of one subset will ripple through the rest of the order; but merely because some subsets of the social order are perverse does not mean all subsets will be characterized by the same coordination-disrupting incentives.

Until about the Progressive era, nearly all public assistance was provided at a very local level, which allowed for a close connection between the funders of that assistance and those they were funding (see Himmelfarb 1991; Olasky 1994; Katz 1996). The contractarian ideal was closely approximated in this setting (see Brennan and Buchanan 1985). In the Progressive era, the role of government in society began to change, and more than in any previous era, people began considering public servants to be well equipped to handle social affairs—including aid provision. Though the 1860s saw the passage of legislation providing Civil War pensions at the federal level, this was really the only federal public-aid legislation that had existed at the time Progressive ideology began to capture the American imagination. Though it was not until the 1930s and the passage of the New Deal programs that the welfare state significantly expanded, the Progressive era shaped the intellectual environment in which public decision making would be made for decades to come. The Progressives sought to approach social problems in a scientific manner, and thought professionalizing the civil service would help rationalize the provision of aid to the poor. At the end of the Progressive era, as part of his presidential campaign Warren Harding even proposed establishing a federal department of public welfare (Tanner 1996, 40). Though Congress ultimately rejected the proposal, the seeds were sown for an ever-larger role for government actors in the public aid arena.

Even when the New Deal legislation of the 1930s was passed, Americans on the whole were still largely hostile to providing public aid indiscriminately. Yet over time, more and more people have come to accept a larger role of the state in alleviating the problems of want and misery. This gradual acceptance has created opportunities for government actors and agencies to continually expand the scale and scope of public aid. As increasingly more individuals have come to have an interest in expanding the public system, the system has expanded to meet this demand. In this respect, the passage of President Johnson's Great Society legislation in the 1960s is just one notable milestone in the march toward ever-more government public aid provision.

The key problem is that the incentives created by the system have evolved to make aid receipt ever more attractive relative to work. Phelps (2013), for example, documents how the expansion of public-assistance programs since the 1960s has significantly decreased American dynamism. While the stated aim of these programs is to improve the distribution of income, these programs also affect the amount of income that people earn in society, as well as the output that they generate. Public-assistance programs impact both current and potential workers. High implicit tax rates mean that those receiving assistance would have to receive a large, discontinuous jump in earned income to make it pay to take on additional work (see, for example, Edwards and de Rugy 2015 and Maag et al. 2016). Mulligan (2012) blames these high implicit tax rates for exacerbating the Great Recession by blunting the incentives for marginal workers to return to the workforce. The explicit tax rates faced by current workers also make it relatively attractive to substitute some labor for leisure as marginal tax rates rise, since the opportunity cost of engaging in extra leisure falls.

Public ordering in the provision of public assistance has influenced the structure of the social order. The feedback mechanisms disciplining both suppliers and demanders now maintain a level of poverty and aid provision that allows public actors to maintain a permanent clientele. All players in the aid-provision game are affected by the expansion of public ordering in this sector. The private suppliers of aid act in the same ecology as the public providers, so if they desire to continue attracting clients, they naturally must operate within the current structure. In response to a larger role for public ordering in the construction of the social-welfare system, the incentives of the recipients have also changed so that they accept—and indeed, desire—a larger role for the state in this arena.

Importantly, as Harvey and Conyers detail, the current system of public aid is undesirable from the standpoint of many individuals that rely on the system (2016).

The authors travelled the country to interview a broad swath of individuals who benefit from various government assistance programs, in order to determine what the recipients themselves think of the current public aid system. The common theme that emerged from these interviews was that:

whether [aid recipients] were grateful for the help or not – they all felt the system was broken. We did not meet a single recipient who had anything positive to say about the programs they were on, aside from the fact of the assistance itself. The stories people told us were rife with examples of redundancy, incompetence, fraud, and general decay and disarray, reflecting programs that are unresponsive, inflexible, and illogical (ibid. xviii).

Most of the people they interviewed needed the assistance these programs provided, but nonetheless felt trapped by the perverse incentives created by the system. In fact, most of the people they met actively wanted to work, but the incentives of the current system meant that they would receive less compensation through work than through relying on public assistance. Due to the "cash cliffs" that characterize our current system of relief, unless individuals are able to receive a large jump in income upon moving from welfare into work, it is generally more economically beneficial to forgo work and subsist on aid (see Randolph 2014 and Alexander 2012 for numerical examples of these "cash cliffs" in practice). Not only are taxpayers harmed by being forced to maintain a large welfare edifice, but the people who are being helped by these programs are unhappy with the incentives created by the current system. As the size of the polity has grown relative to the economy in the aid provision ecology, the order has grown increasingly perverse.

Indeed, Miller (2017) argues that the entire way we think about providing aid in the U.S. is misguided, focusing on the deficits of the aid receivers rather than their strengths, and encouraging alienation of recipients rather than community problem solving. After years working for nonprofits that followed the traditional formula of providing cash handouts to those who could prove their neediness, he came to realize that an aid system that truly encouraged upward mobility would need to empower individuals to use their talents productively, rather than hiding these talents to maximize their chances of receiving the needed aid.

What Miller proposes is not a purely private alternative to the current aid provision system, but rather a reformulation of the way public entities interact with recipients. Individuals and families who are in poverty know their circumstances better than any external party ever could. Not only do they know their current financial situation, but also the skills and talents they possess that could help them escape their plight. Most poor families – at least those who are in a position to need aid from some third party agency – exist in a social ecology that includes other poor families. Miller's innovation was to harness the diverse knowledge and talents of these communities of individuals, and have the people in these communities learn from one another.

The employees in his Family Independence Initiative were specifically precluded from providing advice to the families in this program. Instead, Miller and his employees helped keep an online record of what these families were doing, and encouraged families to learn from one another. He encouraged "positive deviance", which in his words is "an approach to behavioral and social change based on the observation than in any community there are people whose uncommon but successful behaviors or strategies enable them to find better solutions to a problem than their peers, despite facing similar challenges" (2017: 115). These individuals, by productively employing their talents and skills, could then serve as role models to others.

What Miller witnessed was incredible. Within 2 years, average incomes of families in his programs increased between 18% and 24%. Savings increased by between 130% and 377%. The percentage of families with side businesses also increased, as did the percentage of children in these families with better grades and school attendance (2017: 145). It must be noted, however, that this program is just one of many within an ecology of other similar programs. It arose in response to failing public programs, and is in many ways a competitor with these programs. The alternative for most families who enroll in this initiative is other government programs that are targeted toward low income individuals. The real promise of this program, and why it is worth bringing up here, is that the results it delivers for its recipients makes it a very attractive alternative to other similar social welfare programs. Though other aid programs – both public and private – act as competitors to this program, the fact that it provides what many would consider a superior service makes it an attractive alternative for those in the position to need its services. Though it emerged in the response to failing government programs, it is actively helping to support a beneficial emergent order, as opposed to the perverse emergent orders discussed in this section. The number of people it currently serves is relatively small, but the potential for these sorts of solutions is enormous.

5 Implications and Conclusion

For Hayek, as for others, the institutional context within order emerges matters. Both informal and formal institutions impact the character of the order. As explored by Baumol (2002), though entrepreneurs are omnipresent in all societies, the institutional environment within which entrepreneurs act determines whether their activities will be productive, unproductive, or even destructive. People respond to incentives, and if the incentives of the system create opportunities for some individuals to profit at the expense of others, for example, outcomes can emerge which are undesirable at a systemic level.

Emergent orders permeate social reality, but the academic literature seems to focus mainly on socially beneficial orders. This paper builds on Martin and Storr (2008) in probing some dynamics of perverse emergent orders. The examination is necessarily preliminary. Yet understanding the role that entanglement can play in creating and perpetuating perverse emergent orders moves us one step closer to understanding these emergent orders more generally.

This paper is not the first to recognize that emergent orders can have perverse characteristics. Indeed, Hayek himself, in a number of places, conceded that emergence itself does not entail beneficial effects. In discussing the evolution of law, for example, Hayek maintained that "[t]he fact that law that has evolved in this way has certain desirable properties does not prove that it will always be good law or even that some of its rules may not be very bad" (1973: 88). The innovation of this paper is in showing that systematic perversities may arise in a system characterized by significant degrees of entanglement between polity and economy.

It is certainly the case that reasoning about perverse emergent orders entails some value judgements. Within the current public aid edifice, if we take the desired ends of public actors as given, the outcome of the public aid process is pernicious. Their stated goal is to reduce poverty, while simultaneously creating a safety net that helps the poor and downtrodden without creating incentives to abuse the system. Putting aside the question of whether these goals are incompatible, we can question whether these stated goals capture the full reality of what legislators, bureaucrats, and other social reformers are looking to achieve. If we take as a starting point that these reformers would like to achieve a society of free and responsible individuals, then the social order created by public assistance programs is clearly perverse. However, if we take as a starting point that social reformers consider themselves better able to make decisions for the poor than the poor themselves, then the observed outcome would not be considered perverse. Here, I have taken only the stated ends as given; but if we incorporate these unstated valuational presuppositions into the analysis, the framework is considerably complicated. This is a clear avenue for future research.

References

Alexander, G. D. (2012). *Welfare's failure and the solution*. Presentation for the American Enterprise Institute, July 2012. Available online at: http://www.aei.org/wp-content/uploads/2012/07/-alexander-presentation_10063532278.pdf

Angner, E. (2004). Did Hayek commit the naturalistic fallacy? *Journal of the History of Economic Thought, 26*, 349–361.

Brennan, G., & Buchanan, J. M. (1985). *The reason of rules: Constitutional political economy*. Indianapolis: Liberty Fund.

Caldwell, B. J. (2000). The emergence of Hayek's ideas on cultural evolution. *Review of Austrian Economics, 13*, 5–22.

Edwards, Chris, and Veronique de Rugy. (2015). "Earned income tax credit: Small benefit, large costs." Cato Institute tax and budget bulletin no. 73.

Harvey, P., & Conyers, L. (2016). *The human cost of welfare: How the system hurts the people it's supposed to help*. Santa Barbara: Praeger.

Hayek, F. A. (1945). The use of knowledge in society. *The American Economic Review, 35*(4), 519–530.

Hayek, F. A. (1973). *Law, legislation, and liberty, volume 1: Rules and order*. Chicago: The University of Chicago Press.

Hayek, F. A. (1976[1944]). *The road to serfdom*. Chicago: University of Chicago Press.

Himmelfarb, G. (1991). *Poverty and compassion: The moral imagination of the late Victorians*. New York: Alfred a Knopf.

Horwitz, S., & Koppl, R. (2014). *Advances in Austrian economics, volume 18: Entangled political economy*. Emerald Group Publishing.

Hughes, J. R. T. (1977). *The governmental habit: Economic controls from colonial times to the present*. New York: Basic Books.
Ikeda, S. (1997). *Dynamics of the mixed economy: Toward a theory of interventionism*. New York: Routledge.
Ikeda, S. (2005). The dynamics of interventionism. In P. Kurrild-Klitgaard (Ed.), *Advances in Austrian economics, volume 8: The dynamics of intervention: Regulation and redistribution in the mixed economy* (pp. 21–58). New York: Elsevier.
Katz, M. B. (1996). *In the shadow of the poorhouse: A social history of welfare in America*. New York: Basic Books.
Kirzner, I. M. (1985). The perils of regulation. In I. M. Kirzner (Ed.), *Discovery and the capitalist process*. Chicago: University of Chicago Press.
Leeson, Peter T., and Paola A. Suarez. 2015. "Superstition and self-governance." New Thinking in Austrian Political Economy. Emerald Group Publishing Limited. 47–66.
Lewis, P. (2012). Emergent properties in the work of Friedrich Hayek. *Journal of Economic Behavior & Organization, 82*(2–3), 368–378.
Maag, E., Peters, H. E., & Edelstein, S. (2016). Increasing family complexity and volatility: The difficulty in determining child tax benefits. Tax Policy Center.
Mandeville, B. (1989[1714). *The fable of the bees*. London: Penguin UK.
Martin, N. P., & Storr, V. H. (2008). On perverse emergent orders. *Studies in Emergent Order, 1*, 73–91.
Miller, M. L. (2017). *The alternative: Most of what you believe about poverty is wrong*. Morrisville, NC: Lulu Publishing Services.
Mises, L. (1977[1929). *A critique of interventionism*. New Rochelle: Arlington House.
Mises, L. (1998[1940). *Interventionism: An economic analysis*. Irvington-on-Hudson: The Foundation for Economic Education.
Mulligan, C. B. (2012). *The redistribution recession: How labor market distortions contracted the economy*. Oxford University Press.
New York Times. (2008). President Bush's Speech to the Nation on the Economic Crisis. September 24, 2008. Available online at: https://www.nytimes.com/2008/09/24/business/economy/24text-bush.html
Olasky, M. (1994). *The tragedy of American compassion*. New York: Regnery Publishing.
Patrick, M., & Wagner, R. E. (2015). From mixed economy to entangled political economy: A Paretian social-theoretic orientation. *Public Choice, 164*(1–2), 103–116.
Phelps, E. S. (2013). *Mass flourishing: How grassroots innovation created jobs, challenge, and change*. Princeton: Princeton University Press.
Randolph, Erik. (2014). "Modeling potential income and welfare-assistance benefits in Illinois." Illinois Policy Institute Special Report
Smith, A., Wagner, R. E., & Yandle, B. (2011). A theory of entangled political economy, with application to TARP and NRA. *Public Choice, 148*(1–2), 45–66.
Tanner, M. (1996). *The end of welfare: Fighting poverty in the civil society*. Washington, DC: Cato Institute.
Wagner, R. E. (2009). Property, state, and entangled political economy. In W. Schäfer, A. Schneider, & T. Thomas (Eds.), *Markets and politics: Insights from a political economy perspective* (pp. 37–49). Marburg: Metropolis.
Wagner, R. E. (2010). *Mind, society, and human action: Time and knowledge in a theory of social-economy*. New York: Routledge.
Wagner, R. E. (2014). Entangled political economy: A keynote address. In S. Horwitz & R. Koppl (Eds.), *Advances in Austrian economics, volume 18: Entangled political economy* (pp. 15–36). Emerald Group Publishing.
Wagner, R. E. (2016). *Politics as a peculiar business: Insights from a theory of entangled political economy*. Edward Elgar Publishing.
Whitman, D. G. (1998). Hayek contra Pangloss on evolutionary systems. *Constitutional Political Economy, 9*, 45–66.

The Tax Code as an Emergent Phenomenon

Jeremy Horpedahl

Abstract Tax systems are the primary means of financing government spending and activity. Public finance economists have developed a number of rules and principles over time for optimal tax practices. However, few governments rely primarily, if at all, on these rules and principles in their tax code. I argue that this is because tax codes are emergent phenomena, and a snapshot of the tax code at any moment reveals the outcome of an ongoing process to satisfy the desires of many competing interest groups. Furthermore, tax reform, an attempt to "clean up" a messy tax code, is itself an emergent process. Knowing this helps us understand why tax reform processes rarely move tax codes closer to the economists' ideal.

Keywords Emergence · Tax code · Tax reform

1 Tax Policy from the Perspective of Economists vs. Policymakers

Public finance economists agree widely on issues related to taxes. Starting from a basic assumption of no externalities or Samuelsonian public goods, the ideal taxes are zero from an efficiency perspective. Recognizing that externalities and public goods exist, there is an economic case for government spending and thus taxes, but economists once again agree on the method of implementing taxes: they should be implemented so as to minimize deadweight loss. This implies first implementing taxes on more inelastic activities, then moving to other activities, but always keeping all rates as low as possible to minimize deadweight loss, formalized in statements such as the Ramsey Rule for commodity taxation. Adding in the equity-efficiency tradeoff complicates matters somewhat, but still economists have developed a framework for common dialogue, with principles such as horizontal and vertical equity, and the benefit and ability-to-pay principles. These principles can be found in any undergraduate public finance textbook (Gruber 2007, 513–605; Holcombe 2006, 201–242; Hyman 2014, 370–431 and 472–497).

J. Horpedahl (✉)
University of Central Arkansas, Conway, AR, USA
e-mail: jhorpedahl@uca.edu

D. J. Hebert, D. W. Thomas (eds.), *Emergence, Entanglement, and Political Economy*, Studies in Public Choice 38, https://doi.org/10.1007/978-3-030-56088-1_8

Tax policy in the real world diverges widely from these agreed on principles in numerous ways.[1]. A few examples will illustrate this. The US federal government derives almost all of its revenue from income taxes, even though the same amount of revenue could be derived at much lower rates using a broader range of taxes such as consumption and property taxes. The variation in tax systems across states is also illustrative: five states have no sales tax; nine states have no income tax for personal wage income; and while all states have a property tax (often at the local level), the effective rate in the highest state is 8.5 times that of the lowest state (with states scattering in between the highest and lowest). Some of the variation in tax rates across states could be explained by differences in elasticities across states or tax competition, but most of it demands another explanation.

Furthermore, exemptions to taxes in US states often do the exact opposite of what principles of efficient taxation would suggest. For example, all but three states with a sales tax provide some lower rate, tax credit, or have no tax on groceries. This is often justified because groceries are said to be a necessity, but a necessity by definition has a very inelastic demand curve. Given that they are demanded inelastically, groceries should be taxed at a higher rate, though principles of tax simplicity might suggest taxing all goods at the same rate. Perhaps an equity argument could be made for taxing groceries at a lower rate, but taxes are a very blunt tool for achieving an equity goal since the exemption applies across the income distribution, not just for poor household (three states do have a tax credit targeted at poor households, instead of a blanket exemption, and Hawaii has a credit for poor and middle income households).

This divergence between taxation in theory and practice is often evident in undergraduate public finance textbooks. Textbooks will typically have several chapters on tax theory, and then separate chapters describing actual tax systems, but there is often little connection between the two subjects. One could read the textbook sections on taxation in practice and come away with no unifying principles about what taxes should look like in practice, at least according to most public finance economists.

Why is this so? Several explanations are possible. It is typical to blame special interests, lobbying, and generally rent seeking for the divergence between tax policy in theory and in practice. Certain groups are able to exert political influence and achieve policy outcomes that harm the general public, competing interest groups, or both. Undoubtedly this is true. But not all tax policy has an easy rent seeking explanation. Another possibility is that politicians and their staff simply view all tax choices as preferences, and whoever happens to be in office will impose their preferences subject to the constitutional and legal constraints they face. This explanation also has merit, though tax policy as a whole is quite stable in most states, suggesting something other than simply preferences of the current holders of political office is driving tax policy.

[1]Though see Mankiw et al. 2009 for ways that the tax code conforms to optimal tax theory.

In this paper I present an alternative explanation for the divergence between tax theory and tax policy. In doing so, I follow in the footsteps of Knut Wicksell who, as Hebert and Wagner (2013) argue, takes an explanatory approach, rather than a statecraft approach to public finance. Hebert and Wagner also argue that Wicksell's framework has many applications for understanding taxation in the way I seek to do in this paper. By thinking of politics, and more specifically taxation, as a spontaneous order (Hebert (2019), I build on this Wicksellian public finance tradition.

Systems of taxation should not be thought of as a policy that is put in place from above, as if from a single central planner. Instead, tax systems should be viewed as an emergent outcome of the political process containing many different provisions that reflect the preferences of different actors and groups in society, even if there are no unifying principles for the overall system (see also Paul 1997 on this point). To be sure, rent-seeking special interests, as well as preferences for particular views of equity, are a part of this process, but these can coexist along with other forces in a system or network of various nodes of power.

If we look at major changes to the tax system that have occurred over time, it becomes quite clear that no one person or group sat down at one particular time and planned the tax code. It not only emerges from the interaction of various actors, it emerges over time and in response to real world changes.

Thinking about tax systems as a network of nodes helps us to better understand where tax policy comes from, but it can also help us to understand where it may, or may not, go in the future. As an example, I will discuss case studies of attempts at tax reform in the United States. Tax reform is an attempt to change the particulars of a system of taxation, and the language of reform proceeds as if it is a top-down process. But tax reform itself is an emergent phenomenon, though it may be a process which shifts focus and power to a different set of nodes in the network than those that determine the normal operations of the political system. Thus, while tax reform does hold out the possibility of changing the tax system in some fundamental way, it is still best understood as a bottom-up process. This perspective on tax policy can explain why truly fundamental tax reform is rare, though there are many examples of modifying tax rates slightly, eliminating or adding exemptions, and adding or subtracting small taxes to the system.

2 Evolution of the Federal Tax Code in the United States

Where does a tax code come from? The simple answer is that it is a product of the normal legislative and constitutional process. For example, in the United States prior to 1913 there was no federal tax on income. Then, Congress thought they needed a new source of revenue and proposed the Sixteenth Amendment which was ratified by the states and passed by congress as the Revenue Act of 1913 establishing an income tax, which we have to this day.

But this simple history misses many important nuances. First, there were several prior attempts to tax income in the US. Most notably, a series of income tax bills were passed during the American Civil War, and several years after the War in 1881, the Supreme Court upheld the tax as constitutional. A subsequent income tax was passed in 1894, but in this case the Supreme Court struck it down the following year. And the passage of the Sixteenth Amendment authorizing a direct tax on income took 4 years for the states to ratify after Congress passed it in 1909, a ratification process which was not always clearly going to succeed.

The historical background of income taxes in the US and the process of adopting a permanent income tax illustrate the emergent character of the tax code. But just as interesting is the evolution of the tax code since it was created in 1913. The various tax laws passed under the income tax power were later collected in the Internal Revenue Code in 1939, and which has undergone two major revisions in 1954 and 1986. But the tax code has seen changes every year, not just those years of major reform and re-codification. Small changes can be made through the passage of new legislation or by rulings of courts.

For example, employer-provided health insurance and other fringe benefits are generally exempt from the federal income tax. This exemption is one of the largest in the US tax code, but it came about, in part by a serious of historical accidents. Due to both high wartime tax rates and wage and price controls, Congress first allowed a deduction for medical expenses (including insurance premiums) in 1942, and a subsequent 1943 administrative tax court ruling also exempted employer insurance contributions from the income tax. Following the end of the wartime tax rates and wage and price controls, there was some confusion as to whether these temporary changes would be made permanent. The confusion was resolved with the 1954 tax code, which kept in place the exemption that continues today (Horpedahl and Pizzola 2012).

The health insurance exemption example could be multiplied many times over, but it illustrates a fundamental principle about the tax code: changes, even important ones, happen incrementally over time. And those incremental changes come about as responses to changing circumstances in the polity and economy. No one ever set out with a plan in the 1930s saying that "if the United States should get into a major military conflict, let's make sure to implement wage and price controls and higher tax rates on individuals, so that we can then exempt employer-provided health insurance from taxation, and once health care becomes one of the largest sectors in the economy decades later this will be a major tax exemption that Congress will need to consider in future tax reforms."

While the tax code often changes in what we can describe as an emergent manner, this does not mean the changes are always efficient. Certainly, the changes are not efficient from the principles of public finance economics (as discussed above), but they are often not even efficient for the system itself in the long run because of the path dependent nature of the tax code. Changes may be put in place for temporary reasons, emerging out of the needed circumstances of the day, such as the health insurance exemption. But even as the circumstances shift in a different direction, elements of the tax code which serve old purposes may remain.

The path dependent nature of the tax code, as well as the possibility of special interests inserting provisions in the tax code which may benefit them, are a generally recognized feature of the evolution of tax codes. This feature often leads to calls for tax reform, whereby the old, bad features of the tax code are exorcized, possibly as a way of making the tax system more efficient, fair, simple, transparent or some combination of these attributes. However, tax reform suffers from a related problem in that it is not exogenous, though it may come from a different subset of nodes within the overall polity.

3 Tax Reform in the United States

One of the most famous tax reforms in US history was the 1986 federal tax reform. While sometimes referred to as the "Second Reagan Tax Cut" (following the 1981 tax cuts), this major piece of tax reform was most certainly not the product of Reagan's mind, or of any single individual or group's plans. Instead, the tax reform was the product of the interaction of various government agencies, which were motivated by a variety of different constituencies. The Treasury Department, White House Chief of Staff, House Ways and Means Committee, Senate Finance Committee, and some guiding principles from the President all played a role, but just as important are the private interests that lobbied for and against certain changes (Birnbaum and Murray 1987). What is notable about the 1986 reform is that many of the private interests which usually are successful at lobbying were constrained and often failed to influence the outcome, though not on every matter.

In broad terms, the 1986 tax reform removed a number of exemptions, credits, and deductions in the tax code on both the business and personal side of the tax code. The removal of the exemptions was used, in large part, to lower the marginal tax rates, here primarily on the individual income tax. This type of reform was possible and probably needed given the high marginal tax rates that existed in the US and other countries at the time. But even as the US and US states have moved into an era of relatively low income tax rates, the notion of tax reform has come, for some, to largely mean this process of removing exemptions to broaden the tax base, and using the revenue to lower marginal tax rates.

The committee system in the US Congress is crucial for the passage of legislation in the US, in many cases more important than the actual votes on the floor of Congress. But the committee system, as noted above, is used not just for the passage of legislation in the emergence of the tax code, but it is also a major player in any attempt to reform the tax system. Why do committees contribute to the "piling up" of "inefficient" tax changes in some cases, but in other cases they can be the source of reform moving the tax code in a more "efficient" direction? As Shepsle and Weingast (1981) and the literature following them argues, the committee system can be an institution that induces stability for the entire political process, but committees can also be important venues for changing the system as well and producing instability.

Many US states have undergone tax reform in recent years, sometimes with reforms that can be described as "comprehensive," though usually these changes are of a more evolutionary nature. States often take a slightly different path of tax reform than the federal reform described above. The creation by the governor or legislature of a special tax commission or tax force is a common process used, further shifting the locus of power away from the normal subset of nodes in the system. While formal changes still need to be approved through the standard lawmaking process, many states have found that a separate, temporary set of decision-making institutions can provide a very different outcome from standard procedures. Between 2006 and 2016, 28 different tax commissions either held meetings or issued reports about tax reform across the US states (Auxier 2016). The majority of these commissions were appointed by state legislatures, even though states already have standing tax committees which usually deal with tax matters. Other states use special sessions of the state legislature to focus on the issue of tax reform, such as Utah in 2006.

But shifting the locus of power away from the normal legislative process does not in any way guarantee that the resulting changes to the tax system will be more in-line with the principles of taxation that economists agree on. It can certainly mean that the tax code will be different in some important ways, because a different subset of the network of political agents have been given greater power. One key reason is that any changes that are made during the special process of tax reform must ultimately be approved through the standard legislative process. The shift in power is not a permanent shift in the decision-making locus, but rather shifts where the conversation about taxes takes place.

There is some hope that the process of tax reform will result in a new tax code that is at least closer to the public finance economists' ideal. By diverting to a separate process, usually with a smaller group of individuals deliberating, and some of it behind closed doors, it may be possible that certain agents in the system (we can call them the rent seekers) are no longer part of the deliberation process. Thus, the resulting recommendations may follow a general plan of removing special favors to targeted groups and using the additional revenue to lower tax rates overall or return some of the money directly to taxpayers. This outcome is in no way guaranteed, but it is a frequent result of tax reform, for both the 1986 federal tax reform as well as many of the recent changes in the states (Kaeding and Horpedahl 2018).

4 Perverse Emergent Orders?

If a tax system is best viewed as an emergent order, why do tax codes often end up being so poorly designed in practice, even when some of their features do align with optimal tax theory (Mankiw et al. 2009)? Tax codes could be viewed as a perverse emergent order, as discussed by Martin and Storr (2008), who use the examples of social violence and belief systems to illustrate their theory. Perverse emergent orders meet all of the characteristics Hayek (1973) discussed emergent orders as having, but are usually viewed as bad for society from a normative perspective, whereas most emergent orders (money, language, law) are viewed as positive goods for society as judged by normative criteria.

One explanation offered by Wagner (1992) for the US federal budget's persistent deficits is that the budget process is largely a tragedy of the commons. The actors making choices in setting the budget are not the ones who will bear the costs of those decisions. The tax code has characteristics of a commons as well. Those writing the laws and making small changes to the tax code over the years are responding to the incentives before them. The benefits for legislator for writing or supporting a particular tax change could be pleasing blocks of voters, satisfying the wishes of campaign donors and lobbyists, or gaining power through log rolling. But the costs of their decisions will be borne by taxpayers when they pay (or avoid) the taxes, as well as an broader social changes that result from changes in tax law (the emergence of employment-based health insurance is illustrative once again).

5 Conclusion

The failure of tax systems in the real world to align with principles outlined by economists is not surprising. Tax codes are not the product of any single mind but are the outcome of the interactions of various individuals in a system where the locus of power is constantly shifting. Despite this reality, tax reform is a process that many polities have undertaken in recent years and can in many cases move the tax code closer to what economists recommend. But given that tax reform is an occasional, sometimes ad hoc process, in the interim between major reform efforts tax codes will continue to meander in directions that economists cannot predict and may not approve of. The least we can do is seek to understand trends in changing tax codes using the ideas of emergence and entangled political economy.

References

Auxier, R. (2016). *State tax commissions*. Urban Institute. https://www.urban.org/sites/default/files/publication/85021/2000969-state-tax-commissions-2000-2016.pdf

Birnbaum, J. H., & Murray, A. S.. (1987). *Showdown at Gucci Gulch*.

Gruber, J. (2007). *Public finance and public policy*. Worth Publishers.

Hayek, F. A. (1973). *Law, legislation and liberty: Vol. 1, rules and order*. Chicago: University of Chicago Press.

Hebert, D. (2019). The spontaneous order of politics. *Quarterly Journal of Austrian Economics*. forthcoming.

Hebert, D., & Wagner, R. E. (2013). Taxation as a quasi-market process: Explanation, exhortation, and the choice of analytical windows. *Journal of Public Finance and Public Choice, 31*, 163–177.

Holcombe, R. (2006). *Public sector economics: The role of government in the American economy*. Pearson Prentice Hall.

Horpedahl, J., & Pizzola, B. (2012). *A trillion little subsidies: The economic impact of tax expenditures in the federal income tax code*. Mercatus Center working paper. https://www.mercatus.org/publication/trillion-little-subsidies-economic-impact-tax-expenditures-federal-income-tax-code

Hyman, D. N. (2014). *Public finance: A contemporary application of theory to practice*. Cengage Learning.
Kaeding, N., & Horpedahl, J. (2018). Help from our friends: What states can learn from tax reform experiences across the country. *State Tax Notes, 89*(2), 167–176.
Mankiw, G., Weinzierl, M., & Yagan, D. (2009). Optimal taxation in theory and practice. *Journal of Economic Perspectives, 23*(4), 147–174.
Martin, N. P., & Storr, V. H. (2008). On perverse emergent orders. *Studies in Emergent Order, 1*, 73–91.
Paul, D. L. (1997). The sources of tax complexity: How much simplicity can fundamental tax reform achieve. *North Carolina Law Review, 76*(1), 151–221.
Shepsle, K. A., & Weingast, B. R. (1981). Structure-induced equilibrium and legislative choice. *Public Choice, 37*(3), 503–519.
Wagner, R. E. (1992). Grazing the Federal Budgetary Commons: The rational politics of budgetary irresponsibility. *Journal of Law and Politics, 9*, 105–119.

Political Property Rights and Entangled Political Economy

Alexander William Salter

Abstract I contribute to the theory of entangled political economy by showing how entanglement can be characterized in terms of political property rights. A political property right grants its holder a share of decision-making power in a specific context, as well as specifies to whom the costs and benefits from those decisions accrue. Because entangled political economy focuses on the complex relationships that exist between market and political enterprises, theorizing about these relationships as exchanges of political property rights can give us meaningful information about what entanglement is, when it exists, and how it can be expected to develop. I briefly survey the theory of political property rights, show how political property rights within a broader entanglement perspective helps understand constitutions, and discuss several applications of political property rights that can advance entangled political economy scholarship.

Keywords Constitutional political economy · Entangled political economy
Political property rights · Public choice

JEL Codes H11 · P14 · P16

1 Introduction

This essay is a contribution to the literature on entangled political economy (Wagner 2014, 2016; Wagner and Patrick 2015; Wagner and Podemska-Mikluch 2010; Wagner and Rajagopalan 2013; Wagner et al. 2011), which differs in several ways from orthodox political economy. In orthodox political economy, the relationship between the entities known as 'polity' and 'economy' are treated, often explicitly, as additive. One example of this relationship is as follows. The economist *qua* policy scientist and expert giver of advice notes an imperfection in markets and seeks

---

A. W. Salter (✉)
Texas Tech University, Lubbock, TX, USA
e-mail: Alexander.w.salter@ttu.edu

D. J. Hebert, D. W. Thomas (eds.), *Emergence, Entanglement, and Political Economy*,
Studies in Public Choice 38, https://doi.org/10.1007/978-3-030-56088-1_9

to correct it. The economist models the imperfection as a 'market failure' that results *directly* from the choices of the agents comprising the model. Then the economist shows that this equilibrium is inferior to a conceivable alternative. Finally, the economist describes how public policy, such as targeted taxes or subsidies, can correct the market failure and move the market from its actual equilibrium to the more desirable equilibrium. In order for this to make sense, both market and polity must represent an already-ordered set of relationships that are simple enough for the economist to understand and manipulate.

Entangled political economy conceives the relationship between economy and polity quite differently. Like orthodox political economy, entangled political economy remains committed to individual maximizing behavior in the face of scarcity as the backbone of economic analysis. Human rationality is indeed implied by the pure logic of choice (Becker 1978; Leeson 2018; von Mises 1949). But economists within the entangled political economy approach recognize that economy and polity cannot meaningfully be treated as a set of pre-ordered (equilibrated) relationships. Instead, economy and polity both are properly treated as *networks* of organizations. These organizations exist in relationship with each other; social links exist between economy entities and polity entities, as well as between entities of the same kind. Thus, while it is important to have a theory of *order* in the complex interactions of economy and polity, it is unnecessary—and can even be unhelpful—to conceive of this order arising out of the already-reconciled plans of economy agents and polity agents. In other words, there are other, and oftentimes more complex, kinds of order than equilibrium. The great benefit of entangled political economy is that it enables its practitioners to study political-economic outcomes without committing ontological violence by assuming *a priori* that social wholes are no more complex than their constituent parts.

Entangled political economy entails the recognition that market and non-market "enterprises" (goal-seeking organizations) mutually impinge. Of key interest in this paradigm is the nature of the relationship between market enterprises and non-market enterprises, as well as what causes such relationships to quantitatively and qualitatively change over time. Here I add to the literature by showing how the concept of *political property rights* (Salter 2015a, b; Salter and Young 2018a, b) fits within entangled political economy. The "property rights paradigm" (e.g., Alchian 1965; Alchian and Demsetz 1973) greatly contributed to our understanding of the institutional foundations for commercial activity. But it is not often recognized that politics too can usefully be conceived in terms of the definition, redefinition, and exchange of property rights. Furthermore, these rights are not just rights to resources that emanate in non-market settings. Political property rights can be, and frequently are, procedural—they dictate who can make what decisions, and what consequences follow from those decisions. In other words, political property rights have *constitutional* implications. Because market enterprises can sometimes wield political authority, and because political enterprises can sometimes serve as gatekeepers for market activity, political property rights are a realm of analysis for increasing our understanding of how markets and politics mutually co-inhere.

I organize the remainder of this essay as follows: In Sect. 2 I provide an overview of the concept of political property rights. In Sect. 3 I show how political property rights can serve as the building blocks of a "realist" constitutional political economy. In Sect. 4 I conclude by discussing the implications of my argument, as well as suggesting fruitful future topics awaiting study through the lens of entangled political economy, using political property rights.

2 An Overview of Political Property Rights

How do economists theorize about political authority? Within the 'politics as exchange' paradigm (Buchanan 1987)—a broad heading under which entangled political economy also falls—political authority is treated as the result of purposive behavior by maximizing agents who are prepared to offer and accept various "bundles" of collective action outcomes, within a given structure of rules for collective action (e.g., Buchanan and Tullock 1962). But what is it that is being exchanged, precisely? One obvious answer is states of the world: agents participating in collective action are exchanging various obligations (such as tax burdens) for various collective outputs (such as law and order). However, this answer is partly unsatisfying. Within the political arena, agents do not just exchange collective goods for collective costs; we just as often see *some* individuals securing collective goods for which the collective costs are imposed on *others*. Furthermore, oftentimes the nature of the exchanges are such that the relevant traded good is not outcomes, but procedures. Agents trade not just the results of particular decisions, but also the rights to make those decisions.

This is not to say the perspective of the Virginial School is without merit. In fact, the contributions of Buchanan, Tullock, and others are so important that they remain the starting point for current scholarly political economy. In a similar manner to Martin (2011), the way to make progress is to integrate Virginia political economy with a genuinely "catallactic" approach to social relations. This is even more important when focusing on entangled political economy. Given these considerations, we get the best of both worlds by conceiving of political authority as a "peculiar" (to use Wagner's term) kind of property right. Call these kinds of property rights *political property rights*. More formally, a political property rights "grant a share of governing authority and specify the returns that accrue to their holders" (Salter and Young 2018a, b: 5). Political property rights thus specify (a) who is entitled to make a political decision, (b) under what conditions the decision can be made, (c) the costs and benefits that arise from the decision, and (d) to whom those costs and benefits accrue. Points (a) and (b) highlight that political property rights are contextual. Like their more familiar counterpart in markets (e.g., Barzel 1997), political property rights can be thought of as a "bundle of sticks" that grant holders of such rights specific privileges and impose on them specific obligations. Points (c) and (d) demonstrate the essentially social character of political property rights. Political property rights are relational. Unless individuals already exist in some sort of society, meaning they can be meaningfully categorized as having enough in common to constitute joint membership in a polity, political property rights have no content. Indeed, there is no reason for them to be defined in the first place.

This definition of political property rights is intuitive and has many similarities with market property rights. We typically think of market property rights—property rights to goods and services—as defined and enforced by the legal system. But property rights *de* facto can and do diverge from property rights *de jure*, especially in the context of undeveloped formal institutions. Weak or failed states are a salient example. Take a historical case: during the decline and fall of the Roman empire, Roman aristocrats who owned large, rural estates often were forced to accept their workers turning over a smaller share of the estate's product than that to which they had the legal (*de jure*) right. The fragmentation of Roman political authority meant that Roman aristocrats could no longer count on official Roman power to defend and enforce their rights. The aristocrats thus accepted their workers paying a smaller fraction of the estate's produce, in order to reduce the workers' incentives to revolt. Many of these workers were technically slaves, but because of the change in background governance institutions, the estate owners could no longer maintain their ownership of workers. This process, which began in the fifth century, was the first significant step from slavery to serfdom, itself a crucial point in the long transition to free labor (Belloc 1913 [1977]).

Focusing on *de facto* rather than *de jure* rights is necessary to ascertain the true economic and political relationships. In this essay, the primary concept of property rights will rest on *de facto* rather than *de jure* claims. This is true of political property rights as well: whatever the formal decision-making procedures of the governance apparatus, true political property rights specify *who* can do *what* under *which circumstances*. The essay will go into greater detail on this distinction in subsequent sections.

For now, we may ask: How ought the concept of political property rights be applied?. As a way of linking up political property rights with the literature on entangled political economy, consider an example from Wagner (2014): partial political control over financial asset allocation. In a hypothetical free market for finance, one that is as close as possible to a "pure" private ordering (Wagner 2012), the market-level distribution of financial assets is determined by supply and demand. The contents of a particular financial portfolio will be determined by its success in generating maximum returns for the holders of that portfolio. The market serves as a filter (Alchian 1950), ensuring the tendency towards maximization of returns on various financial assets. However, now suppose that an element of political control is injected into the asset exchange and allocation process. A new regulation requires that a certain percentage of assets in a portfolio must be structured such that scarce capital flows to politically favored groups, which by assumption are groups other than those who can employ the capital to maximize returns. For example, suppose that banks above a minimum size (perhaps in terms of total assets or, if the bank is a publicly traded corporation, market capitalization) are required to have a certain percentage of their mortgage portfolios contain loans to groups that have been deemed historically disadvantaged by the political authority. This clearly alters the exchange patterns among agents who comprise the financial sector, and as a consequence, alters the flow of capital and its durable allocations. Whereas previously there was a relatively simple criterion for "success" in terms of what the market filter promoted, namely maximum returns, now the success criterion has shifted to a more complicated mixture of returns and the satisfaction of political criteria. An orthodox political economist would simply model this as one more constraint operating on the maximizing calculus of financiers. But an entanglement theorist recognizes that simply adding one more constraint does not fully capture the nature of the change from a system of predominantly private orderings, to one with significant elements of public or political orderings. The relationships between market enterprises and financial enterprises has changed. This means the *rules* underlying the financial sector have changed; one consequence of this is both market and political agents will have very different expectations going forward over what sorts of behaviors are adaptively beneficial.

What does this have to do with political property rights? The way to ascertain this is to categorize the new financial rule in terms of the four criteria listed above. The rule (a) grants a specific political regulator (whether a legislature or a bureau we have not said, but this is ultimately of secondary importance) the *right* to control, in part, the portfolios of financial organizations, (b) specifies that this right is exercised over banks above some threshold size (thus specifying the rule's context), (c) creates differential costs and benefits for the regulator and the bank—political or ideological prestige for the regulator, lower and/or higher variance returns for the bank, for example—and (d) implies that the rule will be on net beneficial for the regulator, but costly for the bank. Another way of stating this is that the political authority is asserting partial *usage* rights over the capital employed by the bank, but the consequences in terms of *residual claimancy* are retained by the bank. The political body is content with non-financial benefits, such as increased popularity.

We have thus described an increasingly entangled arrangement, as Wagner (2016) understands entanglement, in the financial sector in terms of the changed relationships between market enterprises and political enterprises. We have also shown that this change can be broken down into specific alterations in the structure of rights and obligations that exist between these enterprises. But this still understates the degree to which the system has changed. Unless the financial rule had already been "on the books" and only just now was applied, the creation of the rule did not just give the regulator usage rights over assets to which it previously did not control. The rule also represented a change in *who has decision-making authority* over the rules that underpin the financials sector. What appeared to be a property right to specific goods (portfolio allocation) was also a property right to alter the rules that *constitute* the financial system. In other words, this change in political property rights had constitutional implications, as the word "constitutional" is understood in modern political economy (Buchanan 1990).

Thus changes in patterns of entanglement entail changes in the distribution and content of political property rights. This in turn will frequently have constitutional implications. A theory of political property rights, in the context of entangled political economy, contains implications for the practice of constitutional political economy. To those implications I now turn.

3 Constitutions and Political Property Rights

In orthodox political economy, constitutions are treated as devices amenable to analytical closure. The constitution is comprised of the rules for rule-making; these rules can be amended subject to some agreed-upon procedure; ordinary politics proceeds until and unless exogenous events induce a constitutional moment, at which time the meta-rules are revised according to a rational standard. This is an implicitly harmonious and pacific approach to constitutional political economy.

Entangled political economy proceeds along quite different lines. Although peace and harmony within the polity are certainly possible, tension and conflict are equally possible. Furthermore, some sub-set of political and market enterprises be in harmony at the same time as others are in conflict. Rather than imposing analytical closure, entangled political economy takes an open-systems approach to constitutions (Salter and Wagner 2018a, b). Constitutions, by which we mean the actual rules governing the durable decision procedures of the polity, are constantly in flux, simultaneously being renewed and eroded.

We need a theoretical apparatus that is capable of capturing the complexity of constitutional politics. Political property rights is such an apparatus. First, we must make an important distinction that is often overlooked in constitutional political economy. Especially to citizens of modern liberal democracies, "constitution" typically means the *formal* or *de jure* rules for rule-making. These are usually expressed in written form, as in the Constitution of the United States. Not every polity has a formal constitution, a notable exception being Great Britain. But every polity has an *informal* or *de facto* constitution. This refers to whatever the decision rules of the governing power actually are. The essence of a political property rights approach to constitutions can be summed up by paraphrasing Lysander Spooner (1870): if the *de facto* constitution does not match the *de jure* constitution, the latter is powerless; if it does, it is irrelevant.

Political power follows a logical process independent of our hopes and desires. A "realist" constitutional political economy must investigate this process, both for the sake of pure social science, and for the sake of ascertaining—and hopefully forestalling—worrying trends in the body politic. But because political power is a product of human action, it must still be analyzed in terms of the pure logic of choice, just as is market behavior. The difference lies in the institutions that channel and filter this behavior in politics, as opposed to markets. A body of thought from the early twentieth century, usefully summarized and extended by Burnham (1943), captures this realist element of constitutional politics. These thinkers are sometimes collectively known as the Italian elite theorists, due to their nationality and their preferred subject. For our purposes, the most important of these writers are Michels (1915), Mosca (1939), and Pareto (1935). These thinkers each offer a key insight into constitutions that are implicitly grounded in a rigorous logic of human action.

Robert Michels (1915) coined the famous term, "iron law of oligarchy." His work showed that even in political organizations with stated commitments to democracy and equality, there is a tendency for a distinction between political insiders and political outsiders to arise. Furthermore, the internal structure of political organizations can and frequently will develop hierarchically. For given ends, "command and control" is often an effective institutional technology for getting things done. With increasing political complexity, and for policies hoped to endure beyond relatively short-run electoral cycles, political agents will naturally create quasi-official organizations, such as political parties, that maintain a sharp distinction between ingroup and outgroup, as well as internally rely on command rather than consent.

Gaetano Mosca (1939) wrote about the importance of political formulas. All societies above trivial size and age develop a distinction between those who exercise power and those who do not. In such societies, political formulas develop that justify the restriction of political power to some subset of society. A society's political formula can be thought of as its legitimating principle of power. Political formulas do not have to be false; in fact, they may often be true. Ultimately their truth value is of secondary importance. What matters is the political formula effectively perpetuates stability among the ruling class by legitimating that class and, implicitly, ascribing some content to its membership requirements. While this may seem pernicious to those with strong democratic commitments, it is important to note that without the political formula acting as a pacifying agent, politics would be more contentious, resulting in much higher costs of reaching agreement. In fact, in many societies, (liberal) democracy itself is a notable element of the political formula, despite the inegalitarian political realities within liberal-democratic states.

Vilfredo Pareto (1935) was, in addition to a prescient student of politics, a great economist. Because of the importance of his contributions to economics, his political writings have been unjustly overlooked. One of his most important ideas is the distinction between logical and non-logical action. To Pareto, all action is rational, because it is goal-oriented. But not all action is logical. Logical action pertains to social realms where there is clean feedback between action and consequence. Making purchases in the market frequently fits this category: a consumer spends money on a product because she expects the benefits of the product to exceed the foregone satisfaction that could have been obtained with the purchase price. If she is correct, she is satisfied, and perhaps continues to purchase the product. If not, she alters her behavior going forward to avoid the product, at least if the price remains unchanged. Logical action is analogous to an experiment: in this context, Pareto avers, the phrase "passing the market test" is more meaningful than its adherents know. Non-logical action, in contrast, does not exhibit a tight link between cost and choice. Feedback is messy, and frequently temporally separated from action. Politics, especially in large and complex polities, is a realm where non-logical action is the norm. Political outputs are frequently lumpy, comprised of discrete bundles of multiple goods. And the process by which inputs are channeled into outputs in politics is often opaque. Because of this, there is little direct feedback of consequences upon individual decision-makers, meaning individuals cannot really "test" hypotheses relating their proposed course of action with changes in perceived satisfaction. Because of this, political institutions will not filter outcomes as strongly as market institutions. Agents can quickly learn which market behaviors are conducive to their interests. In politics, mistakes can persist for quite some time.

The Italian elite theorists all tell us something important about the nature of political action. Their insights are abstract, and hence are generalizable across polities. Furthermore, these insights are all readily incorporable into a theory of constitutions resting on entangled political economy. Once again, the key is political property rights. I interpret the Italian elite theorists as claiming there are concrete laws governing the generation, distribution, an exchange of political property rights, and that while the these laws can operate differently depending on institutional particulars, they cannot be voided. Consider another similarity to market property rights. Imagine the state declares a jubilee: all debts are cancelled, all assets and property liquidated; the proceeds are pooled and distributed to each citizen equally. At the instant of the jubilee, there is complete economic equality. Would we expect this situation to persist? Of course not. Because of differences in personal endowments, such as human capital, some individuals would take risks and start up new business enterprises; some would be satisfied to exchange risk for security, taking employment on a fixed wage; others still would drop out of labor markets and enjoy consuming the fruits of their windfall. As economic activity picks up, wealth and income differentials would once again appear. The same is true of political property rights. Even if we declare a direct democracy, eliminating all institutions and ceding all "power to the people," it would not long be the case that one man's voice in the public arena was just as impactful as another's. Individuals would begin rebuilding political institutions and organizations, formally or informally, to advance their ends. Political power would flow to those best capable of wielding it. Political fiat is secondary to the durable distribution of political property rights.

The above analysis shows a strong congruence between informal (*de facto*) constitutions and political property rights. Because political property rights can be procedural—in fact, the ones that are most contested are procedural—political property rights can be constitutional rights. In fact, a polity's informal constitution simply *is* the distribution of procedural political property rights at a moment in time. Mapping out what this distribution looks like is an important task. Taxonomy and categorization are relatively low status in the social sciences, due to its perceived unimportance compared to devising theories with clear testable predictions. This is a mistake. It is very important to ascertain who has what decision rights in which contexts—especially since the possessors of such rights frequently have an incentive to keep that information hidden!—mapping a polity's true constitution in terms of its political property rights is actually a crucial task for the applied constitutional political economist. Furthermore, to undertake the activity of studying constitutional politics in terms of the divergence between formal and informal constitutions reflects a pre-analytical commitment to entangled political economy. The reason such a mapping is a difficult task requiring the specialized attention of a constitutional political economist is due to, in part, the complexities of the relationships between market enterprises and political enterprises. Market enterprises frequently are constitutional actors: although they portray themselves as pure commercial entities, firms such as large and prestigious financial institutions frequently wield their influence to bring about favorable political outcomes. And political enterprises that are not typically thought of as constitutional actors, such as various Executive Branch agencies in the United States, possess the *de facto* power to create new rules, enforce those rules, and oftentimes serve as their own adjudicator in instances of dispute.

A political property rights perspective on constitutions thus enables us to study political power as it actually exists. When a theorist begins discussing the properties of political property rights, and especially when she does applied work that ascribes content to real-world political property rights, she is advancing the project of entangled political economy. In fact, this project only makes sense as an extension of entangled political economy. Orthodox political economy, which assumes a pre-reconciliation of expectations and plans within polity and market, such that the interactions between polity and market are of no greater complexity than the choices that generate such interaction, has no room for political property rights to do any work. Political property rights in that framework could only be the policy itself, as executed by agents for whom there are no disagreements concerning who may decide what, and in which contexts. Thus there is no increased understanding by categorizing the action-reaction of polity-market in terms of political property rights. The project I have spent the last two sections describing, which can justly be called "forensic constitutionalism," adopts the entanglement framework by necessity.

4 The Future of Political Property Rights and Entangled Political Economy

I have argued that entangled political economy, as a framework for investigating the relationship between commerce and politics, can and should incorporate political property rights explicitly into its analyses. An entangled political economy does not presuppose that there exists a pre-reconciliation of expectations and plans among the various enterprises that inhabit commercial and political spheres. As such, market and polity are best conceived as a network of overlapping relationships. Political property rights can help ascribe empirical content to these relationships, as well as formally categorize the lines along which entanglement proceeds.

There are several lines of research within entangled political economy where incorporation of political property rights can significantly advance the analysis. Perhaps the most obvious pertains to the dynamics of entanglement. We understand, in the abstract, that political-economic arrangements can be more or less entangled. And we also have a decent understanding of what more entangled and less entangled look like. What we lack is a description of the process by which entanglement (or *dis*entanglement) proceeds. How does a system where political enterprises exist in relationship mainly with other political enterprises, and market enterprises exist in relationship mainly with other market enterprises, develop into a system where there are many overlapping relationships between political and market enterprises?

The answer immediately suggested in terms of the above analysis is the exchange of political property rights. For example, when a well-established market enterprise lobbies the political process for protection against competitors, and the relevant political enterprises oblige, the distribution of political property rights has changed significantly. The market enterprise that did the lobbying now possesses a share of political power: the right to exclude competitors. It is in effect claiming a property right to the market itself. But the political enterprises are also asserting a political property right: they claim the authority to act as a gatekeeper into the industry in question, and thus indirectly assert a right to the flow of resources occurring within that industry. The lobbying market enterprise has exchanged a fraction of the control rights to its resources to the political enterprises; the political enterprises have ceded a privately valuable (but socially costly) exclusion right to an area of commerce. This example suggests that the exchange of political property rights will proceed in much the same manner, formally speaking, as the exchange of market property rights: when holders of political property rights perceive an opportunity for mutually advantageous exchange, they will engage in such an exchange. A corollary is when the exchange takes place between market and political enterprises that previously were only loosely in relationship, the exchange of political property rights creates a new social link between the exchanging entities. If this can reasonably be depicted as market enterprises gaining a share of political power, and political enterprises gaining a share of market control, then the political-economic system has become more entangled.

A second research area is entrepreneurship. Orthodox economics and political economy has had a difficult time dealing with entrepreneurship. Entrepreneurial activities and characteristics, such as creativity, risk-bearing, and the injection of novelty into market and political arrangements, are difficult if not impossible to capture meaningfully in a world where mutual plan consistency is a starting assumption. Because entangled political economy does not rest on this presupposition, there is room for the market, political, or "hybrid" entrepreneur to act as a meaningful agent for social change. In an entangled political-economic system, the entrepreneur will probably be most fruitfully modeled as the agent that facilitates exchanges of political property rights. This can be captured within multiple existing theoretical frameworks. An entrepreneur must first be alert to potential mutually beneficial exchanges of political property rights (Kirzner 1973). The entrepreneur may also bear the risk associated with facilitating the exchanges, operating within or even at the apex of a hierarchy whose goal is to profit by underwriting such exchanges (Foss and Klein 2012). And the entrepreneur can also be a disruptor of existing political-economic arrangements, affecting changes in the distribution of political property rights that radically upset existing plans and expectations (Schumpeter 1939). Because entangled political economy requires that coordination, or discoordination, be demonstrated rather than assumed, there will necessarily be an important role for the political-economic entrepreneur as the agent that performs this role. Entanglement entrepreneurs will be "loose joints" in the system, but are not unconstrained. They too are subject to scarcity and choice, and they also operate within meta-institutions that structure their incentives and govern the feedback of information that they use to forecast their decisions. The difficult but important task confronting the theorist of entangled political economy will be to integrate the entrepreneur, as a political property rights re-arranger, that neither reduces entrepreneurial behavior to mechanical pseudo-choice nor permits entrepreneurial behavior as a social *deux ex machina*.

The final topic I will discuss is constitutional theory. I have argued that a polity's constitution is its stable distribution of political property rights. We can use this insight to push the boundaries of knowledge concerning constitutional durability and change. Under what conditions will constitutions be stable over time? And what kinds of constitutions are commensurate with widely held social values? These are interesting questions that incorporate a mixture of positive and normative considerations. Especially for those interested in liberal political economy, discovering and achieving constitutions that enable protective and productive collective action, while forestalling collective action, is of highest importance (Buchanan 1975). A political property rights perspective on constitutions suggests that, to achieve a durable and broadly welfare-enhancing constitution, political property rights must be structured in such a way that holders (a) have an incentive to act in the interests of the general welfare and (b) have the ability to resist encroachment on their political property rights, should such attempts at encroachment arise. Salter and Young (2018a, b) refer to the simultaneous achievement of these criteria as *polycentric sovereignty*. They characterize the pan-European (*de facto*) constitution of the High Middle Ages as one that achieved a balance of power among the "shareholders" of the realm such that this constitution can be reasonably characterized as respecting a generality norm (Buchanan and Congleton 1998). Interestingly, political property rights during the High Middle Ages were certainly entangled. There was no clear separation between commercial and political authority, whether in theory or in practice; the various estates of the realm were simultaneously important players in markets and in politics. Yet this did not prevent constitutional developments from achieving an impressive balance of power, which early liberal theorists centuries later would look to when formulating their theories of rightly exercised sovereignty. We thus arrive at an intriguing insight: a high degree of political-economic entanglement does not necessarily result in pernicious consequences, such as widespread rent seeking. Political property rights can exhibit significant commercial-political entanglement while still performing important incentive-aligning and information-generating functions (Salter 2015a, b). Thus suggests the development of a theoretical framework that systematically "predicts" the conditions under which entanglement will be broadly welfare enhancing, as opposed to welfare enhancing for some at the expense of others, is an important work at the frontier of entangled political economy.

References

Alchian, A. A. (1950). Uncertainty, evolution, and economic theory. *Journal of Political Economy, 58*(3), 211–221.

Alchian, A. A. (1965). Some economics of property rights. *Il Politico, 30*(4), 816–829.

Alchian, A. A., & Demsetz, H. (1973). The property rights paradigm. *Journal of Economic History, 33*(1), 16–27.

Barzel, Y. (1997). *Economic analysis of property rights*. New York: Cambridge University Press.

Becker, G. S. (1978). *The economic approach to human behavior*. Chicago: University of Chicago Press.

Belloc, H. (1913 [1977]). *The servile state*. Indianapolis: Liberty Fund.

Buchanan, J. M. (1975). *The limits of liberty: Between anarchy and leviathan*. Chicago: University of Chicago Press.

Buchanan, J. M. (1987). The constitution of economic policy. *American Economic Review, 77*(3), 243–250.

Buchanan, J. M. (1990). The domain of constitutional economics. *Constitutional Political Economy, 1*(1), 1–18.

Buchanan, J. M., & Congleton, R. D. (1998). *Politics by principle, not interest: Towards nondiscriminatory democracy*. Cambridge: Cambridge University Press.

Buchanan, J. M., & Tullock, G. (1962). *The calculus of consent: Logical foundations of constitutional democracy*. Ann Arbor: University of Michigan Press.

Burnham, J. (1943). *The Machiavellians: Defenders of freedom*. New York: John Day.

Foss, N., & Klein, P. G. (2012). *Organizing entrepreneurial judgment: A new approach to the firm*. Cambridge: Cambridge University Press.

Kirzner, I. (1973). *Competition and entrepreneurship*. Chicago: University of Chicago Press.

Leeson, P. T. (2018). *Logic is a harsh mistress: Welfare claims for economists* (Working paper). Available from author.

Martin, A. (2011). The catallactic point of view. *Studies in Emergent Order, 4*, 133–148.

Michels, R. (1915). *A sociological study of the oligarchic tendencies of modern democracy*. New York: Hearst's International Library Co.

Michels, R. (1915). *Political parties. Paul, E. and Paul, C., trans*. New York: Hearst International Library Company.

Mosca, G. (1939). *The ruling class*. New York: McGraw-Hill.

Pareto, V. (1935). *Mind and society* (Livingston, A. and Bongiorno, A., trans). Harcourt, Brace and Company.

Salter, A. W. (2015a). Rights to the realm: Reconsidering Western political development. *American Political Science Review, 109*(4), 725–734.

Salter, A. W. (2015b). Sovereignty as exchange of political property rights. *Public Choice, 165*(1), 79–96.

Salter, A. W., & Wagner, R. E. (2018a). *Constitutional Catallaxy: Friends and enemies in an open-ended social order*. Journal of Public Finance and Public Choice. forthcoming.

Salter, A. W., & Wagner, R. E. (2018b). Political entrepreneurship, emergent dynamics, and constitutional politics. *Review of Social Economy, 76*(3), 281–301.

Salter, A. W., & Young, A. T. (2018a). Medieval representative assemblies: Collective action and the antecedents of limited government. *Constitutional Political Economy, 29*(2), 171–192.

Salter, A. W., & Young, A. T. (2018b). Polycentric sovereignty: The medieval constitution, governance quality, and the wealth of nations. *Social Science Quarterly*. forthcoming.

Schumpeter, J. (1939). *The theory of economic development*. Cambridge: Harvard University Press.

Spooner, L. (1870). *No treason: The constitution of no authority. Self-published*. Public domain.

von Mises, L. (1949). *Human action: A treatise on economics*. New Haven: Yale University Press.

Wagner, R. E. (2012). Viennese Kaleidics: Why it's liberty more than policy that calms turbulence. *Review of Austrian Economics, 25*, 283–297.

Wagner, R. E. (2014). Entangled political economy: A keynote address. *Advances in Austrian Economics, 18*, 15–36.
Wagner, R. E. (2016). *Politics as a peculiar business: Insights from a theory of entangled political economy* (p. 234). Cheltenham: Edward Elgar.
Wagner, R. E., & Patrick, M. (2015). From mixed economy to entangled political economy: A Paretian Socialtheoretic orientation. *Public Choice, 164*, 103–116.
Wagner, R. E., & Podemska-Mikluch, M. (2010). Entangled political economy and the two faces of entrepreneurship. *Journal of Public Finance and Public Choice, 28*, 99–114.
Wagner, R. E., & Rajagopalan, S. (2013). Legal entrepreneurship within a system of entangled political economy. *American Journal of Entrepreneurship, 6*, 24–36.
Wagner, R. E., Smith, A., & Yandle, B. (2011). A theory of entangled political economy, with application to TARP and NRA. *Public Choice, 148*, 45–66.

The Fiscal Squeeze: Budgets Between Fiscal Illusion, Fiscal Commons, and the Tyranny of Experts

Diana W. Thomas and Michael D. Thomas

Abstract The combination of subsidiarity with the principles of fiscal federalism ensures that the government has the knowledge to provide the economically efficient number and amount of public goods without either leaving too much or too little productive activity to the sphere of private exchange. In this paper, we argue that, over the last 100 years, these two design principles of federalism have slowly eroded and we highlight one of the fiscal consequences of this process of erosion: increasing budgetary pressure at the state level. We call this specific consequence the fiscal squeeze, because states have remained fiscally responsible for decisions that are now made at the level of the federal government and, as a result, are experiencing systematically greater budgetary pressures. Empirically, paying for school funding, health care funding, and pension funds, to name a few, has strained the ability of many states to keep balanced budgets and avoid debt or default.

Keywords Fiscal federalism · Subsidiarity · State budgets

1 Introduction

American federalism, as practiced for most of the history of the United States, combines the principle of subsidiarity with the institutions of fiscal federalism. Federated government institutions that operate on the principle of subsidiarity are built on the theoretical ideal that political decisions should be made at the least centralized level to ensure decisions are made by the people most affected by them who have the relevant knowledge necessary to prioritize public-spending projects appropriately. Fiscal federalism is the idea that public goods are most efficiently provided by the level of government that can best ensure that the sum of individual benefits generated by the public good matches up with the marginal cost of production of the public good or service without creating significant external costs or benefits (Oates

D. W. Thomas (✉) · M. D. Thomas
Creighton University, Omaha, NE, USA
e-mail: dianathomas@creighton.edu; michaelthomas@creighton.edu

D. J. Hebert, D. W. Thomas (eds.), *Emergence, Entanglement, and Political Economy*, Studies in Public Choice 38, https://doi.org/10.1007/978-3-030-56088-1_10

1999). The combination of subsidiarity with the principles of fiscal federalism ensures that government has the knowledge to provide the economically efficient number and amount of public goods without either leaving too much or too little productive activity to the sphere of private exchange. The benefits of federalism viewed from a public finance perspective are accordingly twofold: (1) subsidiarity ensures that public decision-making processes eschew the worst sort of preference aggregation and knowledge problems. (2) Fiscal federalism ensures welfare losses from inefficient taxation and spending decisions are minimized.

In this paper, we argue that, over the last 100 years, these two design principles of federalism have slowly eroded and we highlight one of the fiscal consequences of this process of erosion: increasing budgetary pressure at the state level. We call this specific consequence the fiscal squeeze, because states have remained fiscally responsible for decisions that are now made at the level of the federal government and, as a result, are experiencing systematically greater budgetary pressures.

Empirically, paying for school funding, health care funding, and pension funds, to name a few, has strained the ability of many states to keep balanced budgets and avoid debt or default. Whereas in the past federal government grants have been a source of funding, there is great uncertain that the federal budget will continue to aid states in financing programs that were shaped by federal government policy. Either the various state budgets and programs will face much-needed reform, or state taxes will have to continue to rise as a proportion of income.

An emerging literature called institutional public finance or entangled political economy seeks to bridge the gap between static models of traditional public finance and the realities of entangled government budgets. We seek to contribute to this literature by arguing that some of the trends observable in the changing design of the institutions of fiscal federalism in the United States over time are the result of emergent phenomena and the natural consequence of the reality of entanglement of all human institutions. More specifically, we describe two simultaneous trends in the design of federalist institutions: first, fiscal responsibility shifting from local and federal governments to the states and second, decision making authority being turned over to the federal government from local and state governments. We argue that the resulting separation of decision making from fiscal responsibility has created, among other consequences, a budgetary squeeze at the state level. Section II reviews the literature on the theory of fiscal federalism as originally envisioned. Section III defines the budgetary squeeze and details the emergent but systematic movement of responsibility from the local level of government to the states. In addition, this section explores the problems created by federal transfers to states and federal regulation of activities affecting the states when they come with mandates about how to carry out those duties. Section IV offers some empirical evidence in support of the squeeze. Section V concludes.

2 Fiscal Federalism – The Theory

The theory of fiscal federalism seeks to provide a normative framework for the assignment of different responsibilities to different levels of government and for the fiscal instruments most appropriately used for the financing of public production at each level (Oates 1999).

2.1 *Fiscal Federalism and Spending on Public Goods Production*

At the most basic level, the theory of fiscal federalism suggests that the most centralized level of government should be responsible for macroeconomic stabilization efforts and assistance to the poor, because those functions cannot be handled efficiently by lower levels of government. The argument for centralized provision of macroeconomic stabilization is based on the presumption that decentralized levels of government do not have sufficient budgetary means to offer macroeconomic control. The argument for centralized provision of assistance to the poor is based on the idea that mobility would undermine a decentralized system of provision of such assistance (Ibid 1121), because differences in levels of provision would encourage movement from areas with lower levels of assistance to areas with higher levels of assistance (Tiebout 1956).

Decentralized levels of government provide those public goods and services for which a more centralized and uniform level of provision from the federal level would be economically inefficient, i.e. would result in an inferior matchup of the sum of individual benefits with the marginal cost of production of the public good or service (allocative efficiency). This argument rests largely on the fact that because there will be differences in preferences between residents in different jurisdictions and because the cost of provision will differ across jurisdictions, a more uniform level of provision would result in lower overall economic welfare.

From these insights follows what Oates (1972, p. 54) named the Decentralization Theorem, i.e. the proposition that "... in the absence of cost-savings from the centralized provision of a good and of interjurisdictional externalities, the level of welfare will always be at least as high (and typically higher) if Pareto-efficient levels of consumption are provided in each jurisdiction than if any single, uniform level of consumption is maintained across all jurisdictions."

Oates (1999: 1123–1124) explains that the welfare losses from a more centralized provision of a public good will be larger, ceteris paribus, if demand for the good is more inelastic and that the gains from decentralization, while they are dependent on mobility, are not wholly dependent on the existence of Tiebout competition.

2.2 *Fiscal Federalism and Revenue for Public Goods Production*

In addition to the insights it offers about the most efficient degree of centralization of public goods production, the theory of fiscal federalism also offers insights regarding the fiscal instruments used to finance public goods production. Absent monetary policy, government activity can be finance by either taxation or debt. In a federated system, spending at lower levels can furthermore be financed by intergovernmental grants.

The primary insight from the fiscal federalism literature regarding taxation in a federated system is that tax distortions can be minimized if local governments use benefits taxation (taxes raised to finance the provision of specific public goods) to tax mobile economic units and that non-benefits taxes (for general revenue) are best used at the most centralized level of government in order to finance programs that do not generate direct or easily measurable benefits for residents, like assistance to the poor or military protection (Oates 1999: 1125). More specifically, it is relatively well known that distortions in resource allocation can result when taxation of specific and especially price-elastic goods or services results in decreased consumption of said goods or services. In a federated system, excise taxes can create locational inefficiencies when buyers seek out more favorable tax treatment in other jurisdictions, i.e. consumers incur inefficient levels of travel cost to avoid unfavorable taxation. The implication of this observation is that decentralized levels of government should use benefits taxes, the equivalent of user fees, to tax mobile economic units. Such taxes would also lead to a better internalization of the cost of public goods provision and, as a result, a more efficient level of public goods production.

Public goods that do not generate tangible benefits to all constituents, like redistributive programs, on the other hand, have to be financed by non-benefits taxation and are therefore most efficiently provided at the most centralized level of government, which can use non-benefits taxes without creating the above described locational inefficiencies.

Intergovernmental transfers are another potential source of revenue for decentralized levels of government. Grants from the central government may be justified on the basis of arguments regarding the internalization of spillover effects, fiscal equalization across jurisdictions, or an improved overall tax system. Such grants can take the form of conditional grants that come with restrictions on the use of funding or unconditional grants that can be used at the discretion of the lower level of government.

Theory suggests that conditional grants are best used to remedy spillover effect where the use of local services generates benefit for residents of other jurisdictions, while unconditional grants are best used to promote fiscal equalization among the different decentralized governments. Fiscal equalization is empirically and theoretically contentious: while some have suggested that equalizing grants can offset distorting locational incentives (Boadway and Flatters 1982), others have argued that equalizing grants can become an obstacle to regional adjustments that may promote economic development (McKinnon 1997).

The actual design of revenue and expenditure programs in the U.S. case has changed dramatically over the last roughly 100 years. Tax systems initially conformed more closely with the theoretical ideal of the fiscal federalism literature at the beginning of the twentieth century but moved away from this ideal over the course of the century. Interjurisdictional grants were basically non-existent at the beginning of the century, rose in significance over the course of the twentieth century, but have not conformed to the theoretical suggestions of the literature. Finally, decisions regarding spending seem to have moved unidirectionally towards higher levels of government over the time period we consider. We provide a more detailed discussion of these developments and their primary consequence, which we call the fiscal squeeze, below.

3 Definition and History of the Squeeze

Almost all U.S. states are currently facing budgetary pressures as a part of a larger phenomenon which we refer to as the fiscal squeeze. We argue that the squeeze and related budgetary pressures are a result of the fact that the institutions of fiscal federalism at the state level were undermined over the course of the twentieth century. This erosion of the institutions of fiscal federalism was ultimately a consequence of entanglement. At each and every step, individuals acting in the context of entangled political and economic institutions justified changes to institutional structures based on arguments relating to equality, economic efficiency, or expertise. But because government institutions are fundamentally set up to facilitate the creation and exploitation of political rents, the cumulative effect of such entrepreneurial efforts in the context of entangled political and market institutions was to erode the institutions of fiscal federalism with, as we will argue in the next section, systematically negative consequences.

For our purposes in this chapter, there are three levels of government: local, state, and federal. Each has their own means of revenue collection and is tasked with setting spending priorities. In theory, spending and revenue collection at the three levels is compartmentalized and can be analyzed independently. In line with the literature in institutional public finance, we argue, that, in practice, revenue collection and spending on the three levels is interrelated and trends at each level can be traced back to general phenomena dominating the public finance landscape. We argue also, that these more general trends have resulted in what we call a fiscal squeeze at the state level.

The first component of the squeeze outlines the shifting of responsibilities from local-to-state budgets. Since mid-twentieth-century, there has been a general trend for revenue collection and spending responsibility to shift from local government to the state level. The second side of the squeeze is the federal influence on state policy, federal-to-state. This trend is largely the result of an increasing use by the federal government of conditional grants and matching funds to influence state policy. The bargain of adopting federal priorities in exchange for funding has accumulated over time to limit the states' ability to determine their own priorities. The macro phenomenon of the squeeze is the simultaneous shift of local government responsibility as well as financing for things like school funding and policy to the state level (local to state) along with the increased oversight from the federal government through mandates for the execution of state administered programs (federal to state), which, however, comes only with limited financial support.

Relatively straightforward fiscal models historically conformed with the theoretical suggestions of the fiscal federalism literature and taxed non-mobile input factor, which had the added consequence of constraining the ability of politicians at the state and local level to increase expenditure. In Nebraska, as in many other states, the sole source of revenue for both state and local governments were property taxes. From the perspective of taxpayers, spending priorities were clearly divided and attributable to either state or local portions of the property tax and prevented the state from taking on tasks that were local in nature.

This system was undone as the state took on more responsibilities and expanded its ability to tax using an income tax and a sales tax. Concerns about equity in the middle of the twentieth century both at the federal and state level justified a movement away from a constrained fiscal model and aggravated problems associated with the fiscal commons. Ultimately the revenue and spending models were changed so substantially that the budget was placed on an unsustainable path. We argue that this phenomenon is generalizable to all states.

3.1 Local to State: The First Part of the Squeeze

The fiscal situation in most communities and states at the beginning of the twentieth century was relatively healthy. Revenue was usually sourced from one specific tax (usually property tax), which was easily observable for taxpayers and therefore provided transparency. Wagner (2012) suggests that this simplistic approach to revenue collection was useful in terms of disciplining the "fiscal commons." By providing a transparent way of collecting revenue, expenditure items have to be attributed to state or local spending. Schools were local, paying for a state capitol building was a state expenditure, for example. Starting in the middle of the twentieth century, and largely following trends at the national level and among other states, this constraint was undermined as part of a large movement toward what became known as the "Great Society" programs associated with President Lyndon B. Johnson. Concerns about equity and arguments about spillover effects provided impetus for increased expenditure. Coupled with politicians concerned about re-election, this push for increasing government involvement in the economy created great pressure for governance structures to cover larger areas and populations and for revenue models to become more complex.

The erosion of local governance structures within the federalist system of the United States was at least partially based on arguments regarding spillover effects of public expenditures. Around the second half of the twentieth century, the advent of the automobile had made it possible for people to live and work in different communities, which created the suburban landscape of homes and shopping malls as well as the urban landscape of offices and restaurants we know today. In a world with cars, local amenities financed by local property taxes started to benefit non-payers from neighboring communities and there was a particularly difficult mismatch of who funded and who used amenities between urban and suburban communities. As a result, of this general trend, arguments suggesting that the size of the area optimally governed by a single local governance organization had grown became more frequent and state governments started cross-subsidizing local amenities with state tax revenues. Similarly, municipalities started annexing each other resulting in governance structures governing larger areas with larger populations. Overall, concerns about free riders from other communities consuming locally financed public amenities resulted in greater entanglement between different levels of government.

With this increase in scale of municipal government come concerns about equity among the populations included within one governance organization. If some residents of a city experience systematically worse or fewer public services than others, calls for redistribution tend to become more frequent.

As a result of greater mobility and resulting changes in the taxation and spending decisions at the local and state level, the existing fiscal institutions were subject to greater problems of fiscal illusion and fiscal commons, which we will discuss in greater detail in the next section.

3.2 Federal to State

The Federal to State portion of the fiscal squeeze has primarily relied on two theoretical arguments and has accordingly been implemented in two slightly different ways. Like in the case of the shift from local to state decision making, one of the major justification for shifting responsibility to the federal government have been spillover effects, especially in the case of environmental regulation as well as, but to a lesser extent, health and safety regulation. The other justification for shifting decision-making authority have been arguments concerning expertise. Since state legislators are often part-time legislators with a limited staff, federal government agencies as well as federal government officials with full time staff have been allowed to assert expertise to dominate state decision-making.

While the argument for shifting responsibility from local to state governments was largely based on positive spillover effects of local spending, the argument for shifting responsibility to the federal government has almost always emphasized negative spillover effects of private action in markets. Intervention by the federal government into matters that were previously considered state issues has therefore largely taken the form of regulation. The increase in regulations by the federal government that applies to state governments did not come overnight, but in order to erode the federal separation of powers, there were a variety of causes that have accumulated over the last 60 years. As is the case with most regulation, most regulatory structures benefit incumbent industry groups and are often sought out by such groups. In other words, they are a direct result of entanglement between markets and the political sphere.

Environmental regulation entered a new phase in the 1960s, for example, when the EPA gained much more regulatory authority over states due to a political crisis over highly publicized environmental catastrophes (Dwyer 1997). The power that was initially granted for a particular purpose, fixing a problem, became a general mandate to set preemptive standards in environmental law. Basic public choice arguments regarding bureaucratic discretion and growth can explain this shift from an authorization to solve a specific problem to a general mandate.

A second justification for the shift of decision-making power from what were previously state matters to the federal government is issue complexity. As states handle a greater scope of issues, state legislators are facing insurmountably high cost of information, which is especially true for part-time legislators, or so the argument goes. Leadership from the national level on issues such as health care policy, educational policy, transportation policy, therefore, provides a level of expertise especially useful for smaller states and part time legislatures. Which such a shift towards greater expertise also comes greater consideration of special interest issues and greater potential for entanglement to become relevant. Where a state legislators attention may be drawn into directions as disparate as plastic bag bans and property tax issues, legislators at the federal level are usually much more specialized in their policy focus as a result of their membership on committees. Similarly, individuals working in federal government agencies can be much more specialized than individuals working in similar agencies at the state level because of the greater scale of federal government activity on any issue. With such specialization comes a greater likelihood of repeat interactions with special interest groups as well, however, and, accordingly, greater traction for all problems related to entanglement.

The tools used by the federal government to influence state policy have not been limited to the regulation discussed above. Another, fiscally more important tool have been federal mandates. Take as an example federal highway funding: federal government grants to the states were tied to two specific policy mandates that specified a 55 miles per hour speed limit as well as a 21-year-old drinking age (Sommers 1985).

The increase in mandates often comes with similar quid-pro-quos, a funding bill that requires conditions on accepting the funding. The fiscal problem of the increasing use of mandates is that regardless of the continuation of the funding, the mandate remains. In the 1990s the exchange of federal dollars for adopting federal standards was enough of an issue that it was studied extensively by the congressional budget office and resulted in the Unfunded Mandates Reform Act (Unfunded Mandates Reform Act of 1995). The term "unfunded mandates" refers to federal guidelines that are put in place and are either underfunded or become underfunded over time as federal resources, initially given for states to accept the guidelines, erode due to inflation or budget cuts. Examples of unfunded mandates include, the Clean Air Act, the Americans with Disabilities Act, Medicaid, and The No Child Left Behind Act of 2001. States at various times have been skeptical of the federal government's likelihood of continuing to fund mandates over time. In 2014, for example, states that did not accept federal funding for Medicaid expansion under the Affordable Care Act, did so while claiming that federal funding would not keep pace with the additional expenditure. The states were anticipating waning federal transfers in the near future. As a result, 16 states rejected the expansion of Medicare in the wake of the Affordable Care Act due to concern over long-term ability for the federal government to help pay the bill.

4 Consequences of the Squeeze

As the previous section points out, the history of the erosion of the institutions of fiscal federalism can be justified at every step of the way by arguments for equality, spillover effects of public goods, or expertise. The cumulative effect of this institutional erosion overtime is to create an institutional structure that biases government intervention in the direction of redistribution towards special interests, representation of elite preferences, and subsequently a kind of inequality between groups that is not easily overcome by individuals seeking to better themselves. This section explains in greater detail how the fiscal structure of government can have such profound effects on overall societal outcomes.

4.1 Fiscal Commons

Over time, as states took a larger role in financing local amenities, public budgets, and in particular budgets at the state level, turned into a common pool resource (CPR). Common pool resource problems occur when a resource is rival in consumption but non-excludable in the sense that non-payers cannot be precluded from accessing the resource. Public budgets are naturally rival in consumption, because they can be allocated to the production of many potential products or services, at the same time, many different individuals and groups of individuals can lay claim to a public budget. Essentially all citizens of a particular jurisdiction, for example a state, can organize politically to institute programs or pass laws that produce the public goods they desire independent of how much money the specific group or individual contributed to the public fund. Because state governments increasingly participated in the production of local public goods throughout the twentieth century, the number of claimants on state tax resources increased which aggravated the fiscal commons problem. Wagner discusses how each level of government determines its own tax policy and sets its own spending priorities. As a result, budgets at each level are also to a greater or lesser extend "fiscal commons." (Wagner 2007, p. 2/3).

At each level of government, adopting new priorities during times of surplus binds future budget makers who are facing a deficit to either end programs or find additional funds to pay for existing policy (Higgs 1987). The task of setting a budget can be characterized as a short-term or static approach to a long-term or dynamic problem. The dynamic problem is choosing among the unlimited possible expenditures the ones that have the highest priority for the constituents and can be financed sustainably. Clarifying the process of governing the fiscal commons aids in setting priorities. Such a clarification moves the focus of the conversation from the static to the dynamic, fixing a sustainable combination of revenue and expenditure over time.

Radula (2010) applies Elinor Ostrom's (1990) discussion of "natural commons" to the fiscal commons. Elinor Ostrom (1990, p. 90) gives eight design principles for governing a commons that characterize long-enduring institutions in history. These general principles, for example boundaries, monitoring, and sanctions, help solve time-inconsistency issues. The developments at the level of local government in the United States, which had resulted in a shift up of responsibility to the state level and a general increase in the size of municipal government and the areas they governed aggravated the problems associated with fiscal commons because they resulted in less clearly defined boundaries, a lesser ability of citizens to monitor the fiscal condition of their governance organization, and an erosion of the local institutions governing the commons as the size of each municipality grew.

Jakee and Turner (2002) provide and analysis of the institutional problems of the welfare system, which they suggest is an example of a fiscal commons. They specifically point out two types problems with the institutions of public finance. The first is the well-known incentive problem, both intended and unintended, associated with the implementation of welfare programs (Jakee and Turner 2002, p. 483). Welfare programs often generate a disincentive to work and have been criticized for creating dependence. The second are cognitive problems in understanding longer-term fiscal patterns and the ability of the government to replenish depleted resources from general tax revenue. Together, these two problems provide a possible explanation for increased spending beyond what is sustainable in the long-run, they also apply well to the example discussed here.

4.2 Fiscal Illusion

The cognitive problems Jakee and Turner (2002) point to are aggravated the more complex the revenue structure becomes, i.e. the more likely it is that taxpayers will suffer from fiscal illusion. Fiscal illusion refers to the phenomenon of taxpayers underestimating the cost of government as a result of complex and not fully transparent government revenue structures. The search for new sources of revenue to fund the expanding scope of government in the first half of the twentieth century created a more complex revenue structure with increased potential for fiscal illusion. As a result, the transparency of the fiscal situation of most states and municipalities was reduced which resulted in overall lower levels of accountability further aggravating the budgetary situation. While the theory of the fiscal commons explains the problem of state budgets on the expenditure side, fiscal illusion helps illuminate the incentives policy makers face on the revenue side of government budgets. James Buchanan (1960, p. 59) pointed out that if taxes are collected in a more abstract form, then people do not see them as taxes. Going from a simple system of property tax to a more complex system of income and sales tax will create cognitive costs with calculating the burden of the tax for taxpayers. Wagner (1976) articulates this argument in greater detail.

Fiscal illusion helps to explain how both states as well as the federal government have been able to collect greater amounts of taxes over time without significant resistance by the population simply by increasing tax complexity. With expanding revenue collection, a more complex tax code helps minimize the perceived cost for the individual taxpayer and results in greater public expenditure (Wagner 1976: 53).

4.3 Expert Bias

One important justification for shifting policy responsibility from local to state governments and from state governments to the federal government is the greater level of expertise at higher levels of government. While experts at higher levels of government may certainly have the advantage of scale, one problem with the justification for greater involvement by the federal government because of its relative expertise is that state legislatures might actually have more insight into the priorities of their constituents on the ground. There is often a disconnect between the particular set of things a state might provide and the types of priorities that are set when looking at the country from a national level. The one-size-fits-all problem of federal policy can be a difficult obstacle when setting policy. Cox and Thomas (2011) take a look at housing policy, for example, and note different conditions that affect setting housing policy for the nation. Each state will face particular difficulties setting policy that depend on geography, weather, population demographics, and other cultural considerations. Decisions made to correct for local air pollution in cities like Salt Lake City and Denver, for example, will have no corollary on the plains of Nebraska, Kansas, and Iowa. To enforce a uniform guideline or rule for the nation would, by necessity, abstract from such local considerations.

In addition, federal policy prescriptions can only be effective with local cooperation and the use of local inputs. Much of the progress in streamlining policy at the national level has taken advantage of best practices in education, health, and other policy, but has been ineffectively implemented at the state level because local conditions do not match the requirements of more abstract best practices.

Finally, because experts are usually of a higher socio economic status and operate within a different cultural context than the majority of citizens whose lives are governed by their policy prescriptions, they may be unaware of the constraints imposed by lower incomes, culture, and educational background that render policy prescriptions designed by elites ineffective (Thomas 2019).

5 Conclusion

We have argued here that as a result of arguments regarding spillover effects, equality, and expertise, the institution of fiscal federalism have been eroded over the last 100 years. A relatively straight forward revenue system which was often based primarily on property taxes was replaced by a complex system of local, state, and federal taxes that can include restaurant taxes, taxes on disfavored goods, property taxes, income taxes, VATs and many more. Similarly, predictable expenditure patterns with straight forward separation of issues into local, state, and federal projects have become intertwined and interconnected through mandates, federal aid to state and local government, as well as regulation. Many of the changes in the institutional structure of federalism in the U.S. were a result of entanglement between different levels of government as well as between the private and public sector. In addition, they have resulted in greater entanglement between private and public spheres over time. The overall result of this trend is that state budgets have been squeezed and will continue to experience significant budget shortfalls.

Acknowledgments We'd like to thank Ben Powell and all participants at the paper workshop at the Free Market Institute at Texas Tech University for their constructive comments on an earlier draft of this chapter.

Bibliography

Boadway, R., & Flatters, F. (1982). Efficiency and equalization payments in a federal system of government: a synthesis and extension of recent results. *The Canadian Journal of Economics, 15*(4), 613–633.

Buchanan, J. M. (1960). 'La scienza della finanze': The Italian tradition in fiscal theory. In J. Buchanan (Ed.), *Fiscal theory and political economy: Selected essays*. The University of North Carolina Press.

Cox, W., & Thomas, M. D. (2011). Expanding housing choices. In *Enterprise programs: Freeing entrepreneurs to provide essential services for the poor. A task force report*. National Center for Policy Research.

Dwyer, J. P. (1997). The role of state law in an era of Federal Preemption: Lessons from environmental regulation. *Law and Contemporary Problems, 60*(3), 203–229.

Higgs, R. (1987). *Crisis and leviathan: Critical episodes in the growth of American government*. Oxford University Press.

Jakee, K., & Turner, S. (2002). The welfare state as a fiscal commons: Problems of incentives versus problems of cognition. *Public Finance Review, 6*(30), 481–508.

McKinnon, R. I. (1997). Market preserving fiscal federalism in the American monetary union. In M. Blejer & T. Terr-Minassian (Eds.), *Macroeconomic Dimensions of Public Finance: Essays in Honour of Vito Tanzi*. New York: Routledge.

Oates, W. E. (1972). Fiscal Federalism. Cheltenham: Edward Elgar Publishing.

Oates, W. E. (1999). An essay on fiscal federalism. *Journal of Economic Literature, 37*(3), 1120–1149.

Ostrom, E. (1990). *Governing the commons: The evolution of institutions for collective action*. Cambridge University Press.

Radula, R. (2010). Governing budgetary commons: What we can learn from Elinor Ostrom. *European Journal of Law and Economics*, (30), 201–221.

Sommers, P. M. (1985). Drinking and the 55 MPH speed limit. *Atlantic Economic Journal, 13*(1), 42–48.

Thomas, M. D. (2019). Reapplying behavioral symmetry: public choice and choice architecture. *Public Choice, 180*(1+2), 11–25.

Tiebout, C. (1956). A pure theory of local expenditures. *Journal of Political Economy, 64*(5), 416–424.

Unfunded Mandates Reform Act of (1995). Pub. L. No. 104-4, 109 STAT. 48.

Wagner, R. E. (1976). Revenue structure, fiscal illusion, and budgetary choice. *Public Choice*, (25), 45–61.

Wagner, R. E. (2007). *Fiscal sociology and the theory of public finance: An exploratory essay* (New thinking in Political economy series). Edward Elgar.

Wagner, R. E. (2012). *Deficits, debt, and democracy: Wrestling with tragedy on the fiscal commons*. Edward Elgar.

Index

D. J. Hebert, D. W. Thomas (eds.), *Emergence, Entanglement, and Political Economy*, Studies in Public Choice 38, https://doi.org/10.1007/978-3-030-56088-1

The manufacturer's authorised representative in the EU is Springer Nature Customer Service Centre GmbH, Europaplatz 3, 69115 Heidelberg, Germany. If you have any concerns regarding our products, please contact ProductSafety@springernature.com

Printed and bound by CPI Group (UK) Ltd, Croydon, CR0 4YY
30/09/2026
02225465-0007